Holiday activities

impact
WRITING HOMEWORK

Published by Scholastic Ltd,
Villiers House,
Clarendon Avenue,
Leamington Spa,
Warwickshire CV32 5PR

© 1997 Scholastic Ltd
1 2 3 4 5 6 7 8 9 7 8 9 0 1 2 3 4 5 6

UNIVERSITY OF NORTH LONDON

Activities by the IMPACT Project at the University of North London, collated and rewritten by Ruth Merttens, Alan Newland, Susie Webb, Ellika McAuley, Kerry Carter and Ros Heather.

Editor Jane Bishop
Assistant editor Sally Gray
Designers Micky Pledge and Lois Sparling
Series designer Anna Oliwa
Illustrations Brian Hoskin and James Alexander
Cover illustration Hardlines, Charlbury, Oxford

Designed using Aldus Pagemaker
Printed in Great Britain by Ebenezer Baylis, Worcester

British Library Cataloguing-in-Publication Data
A catalogue record for this book is available from the British Library.

ISBN 0-590-53380-0

All rights reserved. This book is sold subject to the condition that it shall not, by way of trade or otherwise, be lent, hired out or otherwise circulated without the publisher's prior consent in any form of binding or cover other than that in which it is published and without a similar condition, including this condition, being imposed upon the subsequent purchaser.

No part of this publication may be reproduced, stored in a retrieval system, or transmitted, in any form or by any means, electronic, mechanical, photocopying, recording or otherwise, without the prior permission of the publisher. This book remains copyright, although permission is granted to copy pages 7 to 95 for classroom distribution and use only in the school which has purchased the book, or by the teacher who has purchased this book and in accordance with the CLA licensing agreement. Photocopying permission is given for purchasers only and not for borrowers of books from any lending service.

CONTENTS

Introduction	5
Parents' letter	6
Parents' booklet	7

Reception
Car alphabet game	11
I begin with 'c'	12
Rhyming words	13
My favourite walk	14
Birthday message	15
Who lives in your house?	16
I wish	17
My favourite dinner	18
How did you get there?	19
This is where I stayed	20
I went shopping today	21
Let's have a picnic	22
Pack your bag	23

Year one
On holiday	24
Holiday quiz	25
Draw a map	26
Holiday poster	27
Design a T-shirt	28
What would you do?	29
Stop!	30
What are you doing?	31
Down to the cellar	32
Garden flowers	33
Cartoon story	34
Who's that knocking?	35

Year two
Take a walk	36
Gone swimming	37
My magical tree	38
I accept your invitation	39
Shopping spree	40
Picture book present	41
Model museum	42
Illuminated room sign	43
Number plate names	44
Going away	45
Sundae design	46
Fan letter	47

Year three
Make two lists	48
Draw a map	49
Make a timetable	50
My favourite sports kit	51
Change a verb	52
Invent a word	53
Alphabet soup	54

impact
WRITING HOMEWORK

CONTENTS

Design a card 55
Treasure hunt 56
What's cooking? 57
Change a letter 58
Alphabet race 59

Year four
Pub bingo 60
Strong and weak verbs 61
Be a botanist! 62
Word chains 63
Make a scrapbook 64
What will you do tomorrow? 65
What happened yesterday? 66
Bored games? 67
Words and pictures 68
Foreign dictionary 69
Number plate phrase 70
Write a play 71
What's on TV? 72

Year five
Time capsule 73
Adjective hunt 74
Thanks a lot! 75
One at a time 76
Brilliant barbecue 77
Five paragraphs 78
Design a brochure 79
Summer treat 80
A place of my own 81
Headline jumble 82

The same story 83
Abbreviations 84

Year six
'S' is for zebra 85
Think of a word 86
Scuba discovery! 87
Comic book hero 88
Comparing newspapers 89
Keep it short! 90
Where are they going? 91
Only three questions! 92
No place like home! 93
Local hero 94
Acronyms 95

Afterword 96

impact
WRITING HOMEWORK

IMPACT INTRODUCTION

IMPACT books are designed to help teachers involve parents in children's learning to write. Through the use of interesting and specially developed writing tasks, parents can encourage and support their child's efforts as they become confident and competent writers.

The shared writing programme is modelled on the same process as the IMPACT shared maths which encompasses a non-traditional approach to homework.

This is outlined in the following diagram:

> The teacher selects a task based on the work she is doing in class. The activity may relate to the children's work in a particular topic, to the type of writing they are engaged in or to their reading.

> The teacher prepares the children for what they have to do at home. This may involve reading a particular story, playing a game or having a discussion with the children about the task.

> The children take home the activity, and share it with someone at home. This may be an older brother/sister, a parent or grandparent or any other friend or relation.

> The parents and children respond to the activity by commenting in an accompanying diary or notebook.
> * This mechanism provides the teacher with valuable feedback.

> The teacher uses what was done at home as the basis for follow-up work in class. This may involve further writing, drawing, reading or discussion.

The activities in this book have been designed to enable children to develop and expand their writing skills in conversation with those at home. Where possible the activities reflect the context of the home rather than the school, and draw upon experiences and events from out-of-school situations.

Shared activities – or homework with chatter!

Importantly, the activities are designed to be shared. Unlike traditional homework, where the child is expected to 'do it alone' and not to have help, with IMPACT they are encouraged – even required – to find someone to talk to and share the activity with. With each task we say the following should be true:
- something is said;
- something is written;
- something is read.

Sometimes the main point of the IMPACT activity is the discussion – and so we do try to encourage parents to see that the task involves a lot more than just completing a piece of writing. It is very important that teachers go through the task carefully with the children so that they know what to do. Clearly not all the children, or parents, will be able to read the instructions in English and so this preparation is crucial if the children are to be able to share the activity. The sheet often acts more as a backup or a prompt than a recipe.

Diaries

The shared writing works by involving parents in their children's learning. The IMPACT diaries* are a crucial part of this process. They provide a mechanism by means of which an efficient parent-teacher-dialogue is established. These diaries enable teachers to obtain valuable feedback both about children's performances in relation to specific activities and about the tasks themselves. Parents are able to alert the teacher to any matter of concern or pleasant occurrences, and nothing is left to come as a big surprise or a horrible shock in the end of year report. It is difficult to exaggerate the importance of the IMPACT diaries. The OFSTED inspectors and HMI have highly commended their effectiveness in helping to raise children's achievements and in developing a real partnership with parents.
* See the Afterword (page 96) for details of where to obtain these.

Parent friendly

It is important for the success of the IMPACT Shared Writing that parents are aware of both the purpose and the extent of each activity. Many teachers adopt a developmental approach to writing, encouraging emergent writing or the use of invented spellings. Care has to be taken to share the philosophy behind this approach with parents, and to select activities which will not assume that parents are as familiar with the implications as teachers. You will get lots of support if parents can see that what they are doing is helping their child to become cheerful and successful writers!

To facilitate this process, each activity contains a note to parents which helps to make it clear what the purpose of the activity is, and how they can best help. The activities also contain hints to help parents share the activity in an enjoyable and effective manner. Sometimes the hints contain ideas, or starting points. On other occasions they may be examples or demonstrations of how to set about the task concerned.

It is always important to bear in mind that parents can, and sometimes should, do things differently at home. At home, many children will enjoy, and even benefit from, copying underneath a line of text or writing without paying attention to spelling or punctuation, where in school such things might not be expected or encouraged. The most successful partnerships between home and school recognise both the differences and the similarities in each other's endeavours.

Holiday activities

This book has been especially designed to provide teachers with activities which supply suitable writing tasks for parents and children to share when there is no

school, such as during holiday time. They provide:
- A selection of activities which parents will see as educationally valuable.
- A means of helping children to retain the skills and knowledge acquired at school over the holiday break.
- A bank of graded ideas to practise writing skills.
- A fun way to pass the time on boring car journeys and rainy days.

Selecting the activities

Unlike the usual IMPACT homework these activities are not intended to fit back into the routine classwork a day or so later. Indeed, it may be several weeks before the children are back in class and the same teacher may not be sending the activities home and greeting the children after they have done them! Therefore it is helpful to bear these points in mind:
- The number of activities you send home with each child will depend on the length of the holiday. A good 'rule of thumb' is to send one or two per week, depending on the time of year – in poor weather the children are more likely to be pleased to have something to do!
- Choose some activities which rehearse basic skills or knowledge which the children have acquired during the term and which you would like them to remember next term!
- If it is the summer holidays you may like to consult the teacher who will be receiving the children in September in case there is a particular topic which one of the activities could lead into.
- Over half term send just one ordinary home-based activity and one to do in the car. It is best not to overload parents who despite the best intentions sometimes find that time has flown by! Try to send home activities that target different skills, such as a discussion and a game.

Sending the activities home

Pages 7–10 make up a booklet which can be photocopied in school and sent home with each child to explain the IMPACT writing methods and rationale. There is a space on the cover for the school name. On this page is a sample letter which you may also like to use to notify parents about the holiday homework.

After the holidays

Although it will not be possible to follow up all these holiday activities in the same way as the normal shared homework, there are a number of strategies which can be used to ensure that parents and children feel that their efforts at home have not been wasted and are appreciated.
- If the children have played a game as an activity, play it together in school and encourage them to tell you how their games at home went. Talk about who won and who lost. How easy, or hard, was the game? Can they make up their own version?
- Do the activities at home yourself where appropriate and bring in your versions to share with the children.
- Start the new term or half-term by writing a comment about the holiday activities in the child's shared writing homework or IMPACT diary so that the parents know that you know they have done the homework!
- Do value the work that the children and their parents do at home. Sometimes it may not be presented as you expect – for example, a lot of parents with young children write in upper case rather than lower case letters or will ask children to **write over** a line of print. Remember that what comes back into class is a starting point for work that you consider appropriate, and is facilitating both discussion and partnership between the children's homes and school.

Dear Parents,

We are enclosing some writing for you to share with your child over the school holidays.

Please can you remember the following:

- Choose a time to do these activities when they do not have to compete with something else particularly exciting – such as a favourite film or a bike ride! Your child will put much more energy in if he/she feels that they are getting your attention when they are bored!

- Many of the activities can take place when you are 'out and about' so incorporate them into your normal activities and then provide a little time at home to finish off the activity.

- Be as enthusiastic as you can. A gloomy attitude and a muttered 'This looks a waste of time' can kill a valuable activity.

- Try to let your child take the lead. Allow him or her to explain things to you if possible. It is often by putting things into their own words that they learn.

- We are interested in how your child got on with the activity so do let us know by filling out the homework diary and writing a brief comment if you want. It is your support of your child's learning which helps them to succeed. We value all the help you give.

We hope you all have fun with these activities.

Yours sincerely

Class Teacher

Don't forget...

Pick your time!
When you both want to do the activity.

Don't over-correct!
This can be very discouraging.

Your child does not always have to do all the writing!
You may take turns, or take over sometimes.

Make it fun!
If either of you gets tired or bored help a bit more. Tasks should not last more than 20 minutes unless you want them to!

Praise and encourage as much as you can!

IMPACT

Shared Writing

SPIKe

School name

About Shared Writing

- The teacher selects an activity
- The teacher explains the activity to the class.
- Child and helper read through the activity.
- Child and helper talk about the activity.
- Child and helper share the writing.
- Child and helper comment on the activity in the diary.
- Child brings the activity back into school.
- Teacher reads the comments in the diary.
- The teacher follows up the activity in class.

Spelling and punctuation

We all agree that correct spelling and punctuation are very important. However........

DO

- Notice punctuation when sharing the writing activity.
- Talk about different uses of capital and lower case letters.
- Play word games such as 'I spy' or 'Hangman'.
- Read what the child has written before you make any comment about spelling, punctuation or presentation.
- Help them learn any words sent home by the school.

DON'T

- Worry about every mistake – children can become very anxious about their writing if constantly interrupted.
- With young children don't insist that they spell every word correctly. At this stage we are encouraging them to 'be writers'.
- Don't worry if your child is quite slow to learn to spell and punctuate – these things come with time and encouragement.

How we write

Writing also has a mechanical side, children have to learn to form their letters, to separate words, to begin and end sentences.

When children are first learning to write it can be very discouraging to be constantly corrected. However, as they become more confident, we can afford to draw their attention to certain things.

Developing skills

Your child already knows quite a lot about writing when they start school. They may:
• be able to tell the difference between writing and pictures;
• realise that writing has words and spaces;
• know some letters of their name;
• be able to make marks on paper or form a few letters;
• understand that 'talk' can be written down and that writing can give messages or information;
• play at 'reading' their own writing.

As they get older, children need encouragement to become independent readers and writers. You can help by:
• Talking about the book they are reading – or even comics or magazines. Ask questions such as 'what do you like best about your book?'.

Above all:
Don't shout because they spell something wrongly!
Do encourage them by looking for letter patterns.
Don't mock a child who finds spelling hard.
Do make a SHORT list of common words and pin it up where everyone will see it every day!

Being a writer...

Is about...
Having ideas
Composing them
Communicating them

WANTED
A Purpose
a.k.a.
A Greeting
A Compliment
An Enquiry
A Gossip
A Thought

To An Audience
my teacher
Mum or Dad
Friend or foe
Near or far

Choose from our catalogue of Types of Writing
a letter
a poster
a list
a book

Parents can help by...

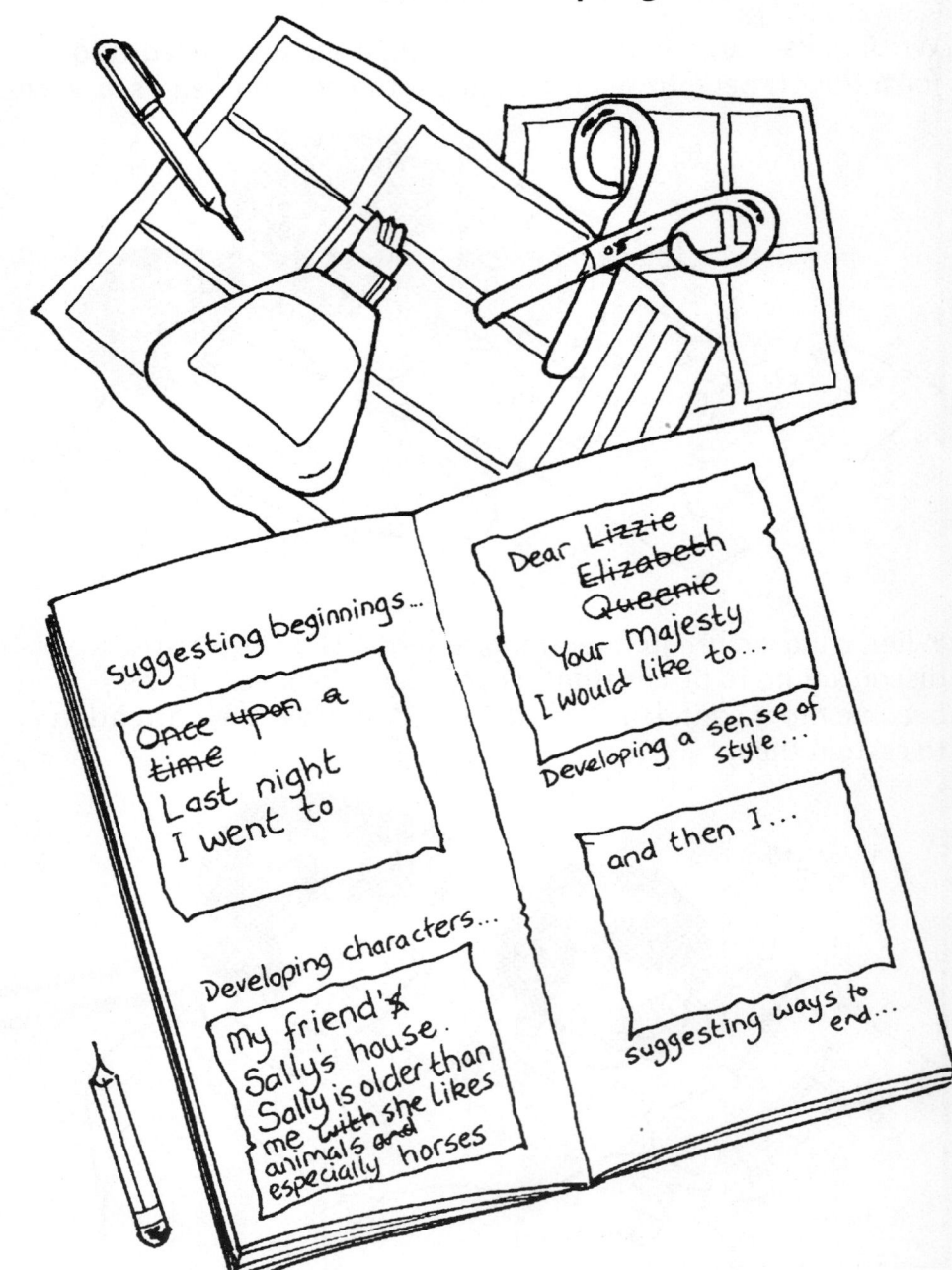

Suggesting beginnings...

~~Once upon a time~~
Last night I went to

Dear ~~Lizzie~~ ~~Elizabeth~~ ~~Queenie~~ Your majesty
I would like to...

Developing a sense of style...

and then I...

Developing characters...

My friend's Sally's house. Sally is older than me ~~with~~ she likes ~~animals and~~ especially horses

suggesting ways to end...

Car alphabet game

- Play this game when you are in a car or on the bus.
- Look at car number plates. First find one which begins with the letter A, then B. How far through the alphabet can you go? Which letters can't you find?

To the helper:
- This is a game for all the family. You may need to take turns and help your child.
- Point out to your child that older cars have the single letter at the end of the number plate rather than at the beginning.

This activity encourages children to learn the alphabet in the correct order. Confidence in alphabet skills will help future writing work.

_____ and
child

_____
helper(s)

_____
did this activity together

Holiday activities 11

To the helper:

- Choose a letter sound such as 'c' as in cat, not 'c' as in ceiling and encourage your child to draw pictures. Point to the pictures saying 'I begin with 'c' said the little cup'.
- Write the words alongside the pictures in lower case letters for your child to copy and read.
- Choose another letter when your child is ready.

Learning letter sounds is essential for children to become confident with reading and writing.

_____and

child

_____

helper(s)

_____

did this activity together

I begin with 'c'

Which is your favourite letter?

● Draw some pictures of things which begin with your favourite letter. Write down the words too.

12   Holiday activities

impact WRITING HOMEWORK

Rhyming words

Can you think of some words which rhyme with each other?

Like this: The rat and the cat sat on the mat.

- Draw a picture to go with your sentence.

To the helper:

- Help your child to make a list of rhyming words.
- Encourage the use of the two sound segments 'c' and 'at' and so on.
- Extend this by using 'an', 'ap' and 'ar' as ending syllables.

Learning to 'hear' rhythms and rhymes increases children's confidence. Children realise they can read and write several words for themselves.

_____ and
child

_____
helper(s)

_____
did this activity together

impact WRITING HOMEWORK

Holiday activities

To the helper:

- Choose a very short walk to take your child on. Talk about the things you see while you are out.
- Help your child choose four favourite features such as a church, a beautiful tree or a letter box. Help to label the picture.

This is an excellent activity for increasing memory and observational skills. Both are essential for reading and writing.

_____ and
child

_____
helper(s)

_____
did this activity together

14   Holiday activities

My favourite walk

● Take a short walk with your helper.

● When you get back home draw a picture of your walk and write down four things you saw. You might have seen a special tree or a cat sitting on a wall. Choose your favourite things.

1 _____   2 _____

3 _____   4 _____

impact WRITING HOMEWORK

Birthday message

Do you know anyone who is having their birthday soon?
- Can you think of a special message to write to say happy birthday? Write it down.

To the helper:

- Children enjoy writing their own cards. Help your child to think of a suitable message. You may need to write it down in lower case letters for your child to copy.
- Read it together once it is written down.

Reading and writing together will help focus attention on a few meaningful words.

_____ and
child

_____
helper(s)

_____
did this activity together

impact WRITING HOMEWORK

Holiday activities   15

To the helper:

● Help your child by letting them copy either from this sheet or write the words out (in lower case letters) and let them copy your writing.
● Read the words together. Ask your child to find a matching word in both sentences (for example 'is').

This activity will help your child become familiar with frequently used vocabulary.

_____and
child

_____
helper(s)

_____
did this activity together

16   Holiday activities

Who lives in your house?

Who lives in your house?

● Draw a picture of everyone who lives in your house.

● Now ask your helper to help you write:

This is me, my name is – – – – –

This is my mum her name is – – – –

impact WRITING HOMEWORK

I wish

- Think of a very special wish.
- Draw a picture to show your wish. Tell your helper why you would like your wish to come true.

To the helper:
- Encourage your child to tell you what they would wish for and the reasons why.
- Help write the reasons down on a piece of paper. Read the reasons together by pointing at each word.
- Stick the writing underneath the picture.

It is often necessary for children to repeat an activity several times in order to learn. Repeating sentences which they have written and which are important to them is an ideal way to encourage this.

_____and
child

_____
helper(s)

_____

did this activity together

Holiday activities   17

To the helper:

- Help your child to identify their favourite food and help them write the words. Make sure any writing which they copy is written in lower case letters.
- Read the words together.

Looking carefully at individual words and memorising them will give your child confidence with reading and writing.

_____ and

child

_____

helper(s)

_____

did this activity together

18   **Holiday activities**

My favourite dinner

If you could choose anything, what would your favourite dinner be?

- Draw a picture of it.
- Ask your helper to label your picture with you.

impact WRITING HOMEWORK

How did you get there?

Have you been away on holiday? Or to stay with your family? Or on a trip to the zoo or the park? How did you get there?

- Draw a picture to show how you travelled. Was it by car, or bus? Was it on an aeroplane or a boat? Or did you walk?

To the helper:

- Discuss with your child how you travelled. If you used more than one method of transport, can they recall the sequence?
- If there is a seqence write each method on a different piece of paper and read the sequence together.

Remembering the correct sequence of what happened is very important for logical thinking.

_____and
child

_____
helper(s)

_____

did this activity together

Holiday activities

To the helper:

- Encourage your child to observe carefully any details ready for their drawing. If they stayed in a caravan, for example, make sure they recall the colour, number of windows and other details correctly.
- Write some labels for your child to copy. Don't forget to write using lower case letters.

Drawing and labelling accurately is an essential skill for many areas in school.

_____ and
child

_____
helper(s)

_____
did this activity together

20   Holiday activities

This is where I stayed

Have you stayed somewhere away from home? Perhaps you have been on holiday and stayed somewhere new. Or perhaps you have been to stay with your grandma or at a friend's house.

- Draw a picture of the place where you stayed. Write some labels to explain your picture.

impact WRITING HOMEWORK

I went shopping today

Next time you go shopping choose four things to put in your own basket.

- Draw a picture of your shopping and label the items.

I went shopping today and I bought some – – – –
What did you put in your basket today?

To the helper:

- When you go shopping let your child have a basket of their own to put four items into.
- Back at home help your child to label the items on their drawing.
- Read the sentence here together 'I went shopping today and bought...'.
- Repeat the activity on another shopping trip.

Becoming familiar with one sentence helps build a child's confidence.

_____and
child

_____
helper(s)

_____

did this activity together

impact WRITING HOMEWORK

Holiday activities

To the helper:

● Help your child to write the labels in lower case letters. Perhaps your child could write the initial letter of the word and you could show them how to write the other letters.

● Cut out your own labels and stick them onto your picture near the relevant items.

Accurate labelling of diagrams is very important as a skill in school.

_____ and

child

_____

helper(s)

_____

did this activity together

22   Holiday activities

Let's have a picnic

Imagine you are going for a picnic.

● Draw some pictures of all the things which you would like to have for your picnic.
● Write labels for all the foods you have chosen.

| sandwich |
| cake |
| tomato |
| lemonade |

impact WRITING HOMEWORK

Pack your bag

- Pretend that you must pack your bag ready for a trip.
- Make a list of all the things you will need.
- Write your name and address on this label too.

To the helper:

- If you go away on holiday encourage your child to pack a small bag with their own items in it. See if they can arrange some of the items in alphabetical order – book, coat, dress.
- Ask your child to write the first letter of an item and help with the rest of the word.

This activity will help your child to write an accurate list and gives practise with the alphabet.

_____and
child

_____
helper(s)

_____
did this activity together

impact WRITING HOMEWORK

Holiday activities 23

To the helper:

- Talk about the chosen activity together.
- Write some ideas for sentences down together. Remind your child that each idea will begin with a capital letter and end with a full stop.

Writing in sentences is difficult at first. It helps to identify separate ideas, each one demarcated.

_____ and
child

_____
helper(s)

_____
did this activity together

Holiday activities

On holiday

What is your favourite thing to do when you are on holiday?

● Draw a picture and write a few sentences to describe your favourite holiday activity.

impact WRITING HOMEWORK

Holiday quiz

What was your holiday like?

- Write an answer for each of these questions:

Where did you go on holiday?

How did you travel there?

Where did you stay?

What did you like doing best on your holiday?

To the helper:

- Please help your child to think of a complete sentence to answer these questions, for example 'I went to France on my holiday' (not simply – 'France').
- Write the answers together reminding your child that each sentence will begin with a capital letter and end with a full stop.

This activity helps to recognise question marks and to recognise the words that are often used in questions, for example: where, when, how, who, what and which.

_____ and

child

_____

helper(s)

_____

did this activity together

Holiday activities

To the helper:

- While you are in the park you might like to discuss the positions of the main features in the park.
- Please give help by drawing a rough general outline shape and marking the entrance to the park.
- Use positional words to help, for example: next to, between, behind.

Using positional language accurately is particularly important in geography work in school.

_____ and

child

_____

helper(s)

_____

did this activity together

26   **Holiday activities**

Draw a map

Is there a park, playground or leisure centre which you sometimes visit?

- Draw a labelled map to show where everything is in the park.

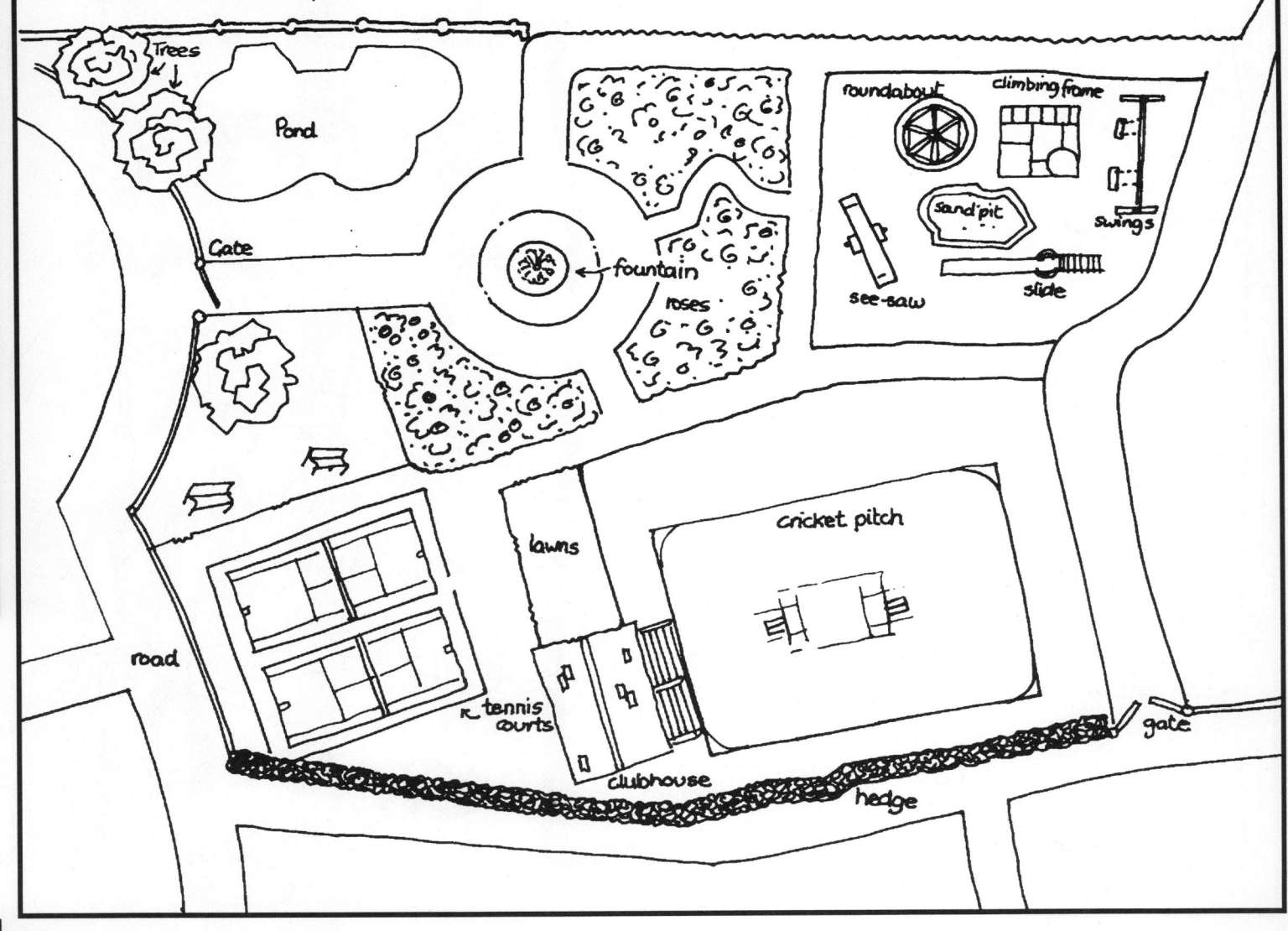

Map labels: Trees, Pond, Gate, roundabout, climbing frame, sand pit, swings, see-saw, slide, fountain, roses, lawns, road, tennis courts, clubhouse, cricket pitch, gate, hedge

impact WRITING HOMEWORK

Holiday poster

Have you visited a new place for a holiday?

- Make a poster about the place where you went. Or about somewhere imaginary if you prefer.

- Remember to write the name of the place on your poster and a caption to encourage other people to visit.

To the helper:

- Talk about the essential characteristics of the place you visited. Which features made it special for you?
- Try to write a suitable caption, collect several ideas from all the family before choosing a favourite.

Collaborating to write a caption will provide many interesting ideas.

_____ and

child

_____

helper(s)

_____

did this activity together

Holiday activities 27

To the helper:

- If your child doesn't have a suitable T-shirt to copy, think of a hobby, interest or favourite book or television programme as a topic. Advertisements or comics might inspire you.

Trying to compose a short, snappy message is very difficult and will use many new writing skills.

_____ and
child

_____
helper(s)

_____
did this activity together

Design a T-shirt

Have you got a favourite T-shirt with some words written on it?

- Draw a picture of it here. It can be an imaginary one if you prefer – you will need to think of a short message to write on your T-shirt.

28   **Holiday activities**

impact WRITING HOMEWORK

What would you do?

What would you do if this happened to you?

- Write a story about what would happen.

"Please can I come in?"

- Think about:

What will your family say?

What will you say?

What happens next?

Do you play together?

What does it like to eat?

impact WRITING HOMEWORK

To the helper:

- Talk about how you would feel when confronted by the monster. What would you do?
- When you have some good ideas write them down together. Your child can write the short words (is, in, the) and the beginning of the other words.
- Writing together is wonderful for confidence building. Read the story together when it is complete.

Writing imaginative stories is an important aspect of English. This activity will encourage your child to use imagery.

_____and

child

_____

helper(s)

_____

did this activity together

Holiday activities 29

To the helper:

- This activity will encourage your child to look for words in the environment.

Identifying words gives children great satisfaction. It also increases their observation and concentration skills.

_____and

child

_____

helper(s)

_____

did this activity together

Holiday activities

Stop!

Have you noticed the different road signs when you are out walking, in a car or on a bus?

- Draw three road signs which you have seen which have words.
Ask a grown up to explain the signs for you.

- Now design a new road sign with some words on. What does it mean?

impact WRITING HOMEWORK

What are you doing?

How many words ending in –ing can you say?

● Write three favourite –ing words and draw some pictures to go with them.

To the helper:

● Please help your child to write a list of verbs.
● Start by spelling short '–ing' words, for example sing, wing, ring.

Learning to read and write syllables gives children confidence in spelling and is a helpful strategy for identifying words.

_____and

child

_____

helper(s)

_____

did this activity together

Holiday activities

To the helper:

- You may like to play this game whilst travelling, in the car, for example. It focuses on the beginning and ending of words – the middle of words are very difficult to hear.
- Encourage your child to think of suitable three letter words.

Being able to 'hear' the final sound in a word takes time to develop. This activity will help your child to focus on the final consonant.

_____and
child

_____
helper(s)

did this activity together

Down to the cellar

These words look like a staircase!
- Try to continue the stairway down to the cellar.

```
c a t
    a
    p e n
        e
        t
```

Holiday activities

Garden flowers

Choose two different flowers from your garden or the park.

- Draw a picture of your two flowers and label your pictures carefully.
- Now write down some sentences to say how the two flowers are different from each other.

To the helper:

- Discuss the similarities and differences before beginning the task.
- Help your child to construct the sentences and give reminders about full stops and capital letters.

Good observational skills are essential. This activity will also help your child to write in sentences.

_____and
child

_____
helper(s)

_____

did this activity together

Holiday activities

To the helper:

- Before beginning this activity you might like to read some comics together. Discuss a character and a plot for your cartoon strip.
- If necessary please help by writing the conversation on separate pieces of paper.

Children love comics and this activity helps them with the important skill of being concise and precise.

_____and
child

_____
helper(s)

_____
did this activity together

34   Holiday activities

Cartoon story

Can you think of an exciting story which could happen to you?

- Draw pictures of yourself and a favourite character in a cartoon strip.

impact WRITING HOMEWORK

Who's that knocking?

Can you make up a story?

- Draw three pictures on separate pieces of paper to show the beginning, middle and end of your story.

- Write a few sentences under each picture to tell the story.

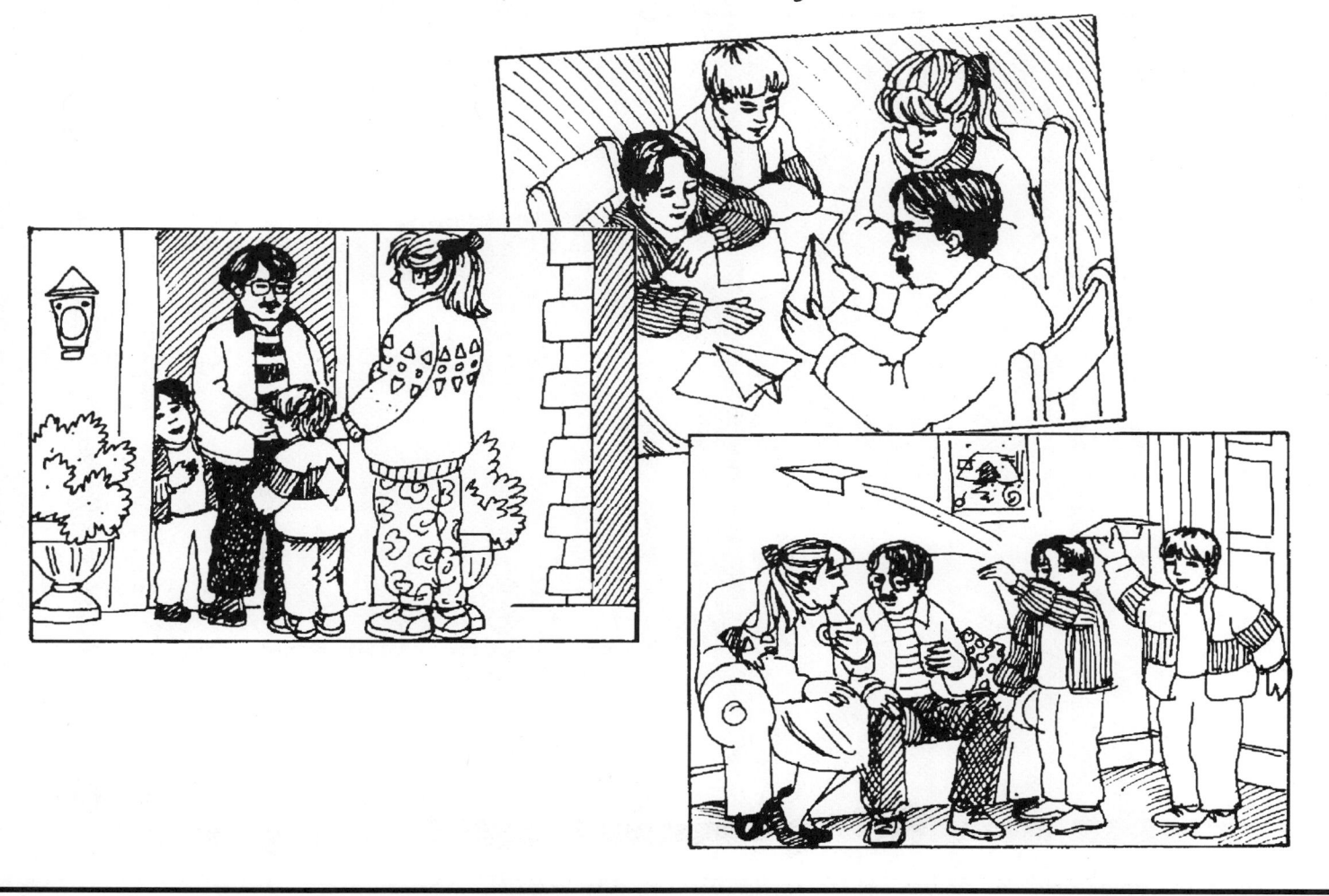

To the helper:

- Encourage your child to tell you their story first. Help by suggesting how the story could move on or by asking for more information. Retell the story back to your child and then write the story down together.
- Encourage your child to write as much as possible but be prepared to help when necessary. Read and enjoy the story together.

All good stories have a beginning that introduces the story, a middle where things happen and an ending to finish the story off.

_____ and
child

_____
helper(s)

_____

did this activity together

Holiday activities 35

To the helper:

- Think about this activity while you are out on a walk. This will enable you to discuss the main features and their positions to mark on the map later.

Being able to draw a simple map to show the main features of a small location is an important geographical skill.

_____ and
child

_____
helper(s)

_____
did this activity together

36   Holiday activities

Take a walk

Have you been on an interesting walk on holiday?

- Draw and label a map of your favourite holiday walk. It might be at the zoo, a castle or an amusement park.

impact WRITING HOMEWORK

Gone swimming

What do you need if you are going swimming?

- Draw all the things you will need.
- Write a list of everything which you have drawn.

To the helper:

- Encourage your child to imagine that they must pack their own bag to go swimming.
- Discuss the list to make sure that nothing has been forgotten.

Writing lists is an important skill in science and technology which will be useful in school.

_____ and

child

_____

helper(s)

_____

did this activity together

Holiday activities

To the helper:

● Encourage your child to tell you their story first. Give help by suggesting how the story could move on or by asking for more information. Retell the story back to your child and then write the story down together.

● Encourage your child to write as much as possible but be prepared to help as much as necessary. Read and enjoy the finished story together.

All good stories have a beginning that introduces the story, a middle where things happen and an ending to finish the story.

_____and
child

_____
helper(s)

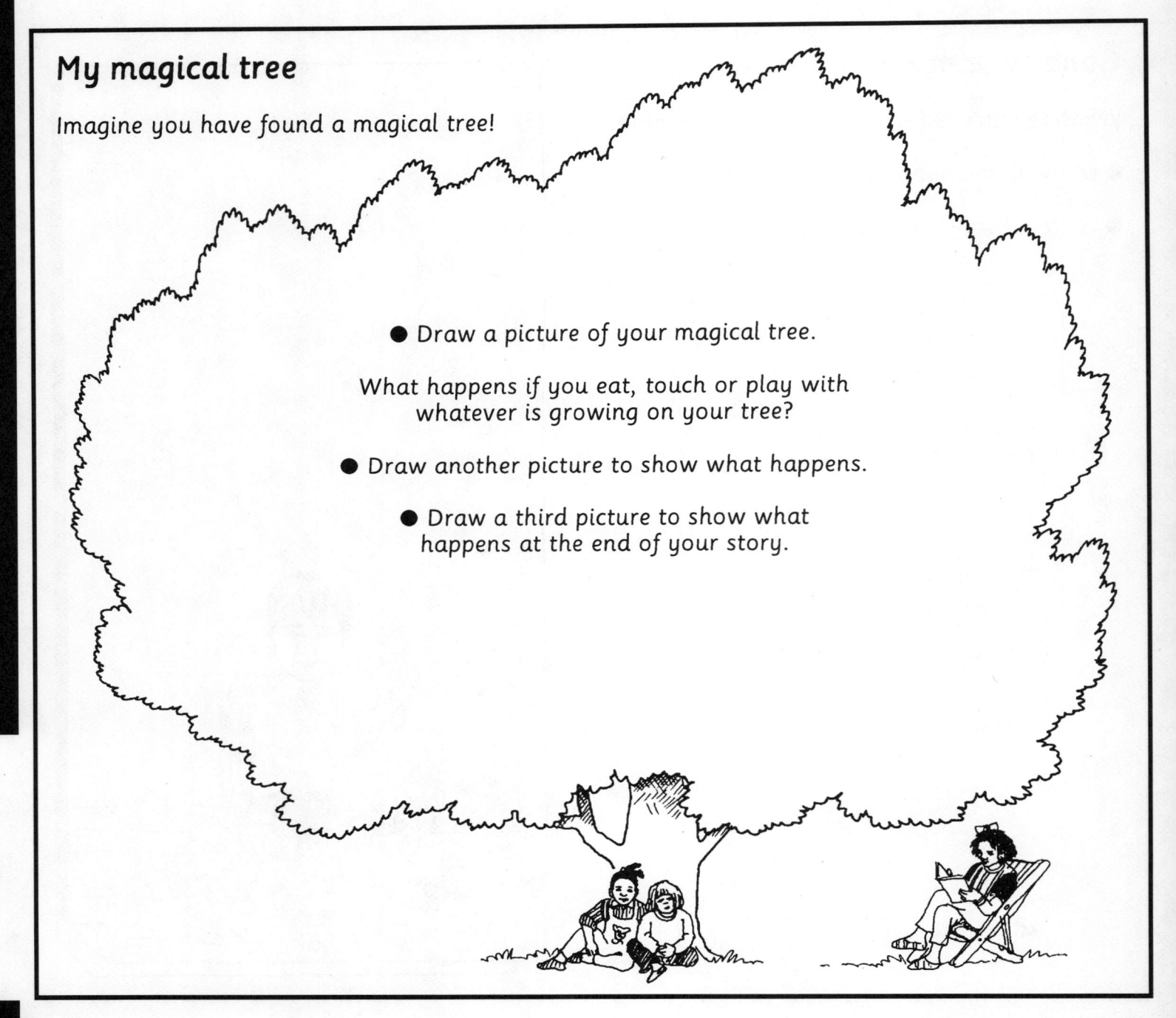

_____
did this activity together

My magical tree

Imagine you have found a magical tree!

● Draw a picture of your magical tree.

What happens if you eat, touch or play with whatever is growing on your tree?

● Draw another picture to show what happens.

● Draw a third picture to show what happens at the end of your story.

38 **Holiday activities**

impact WRITING HOMEWORK

I accept your invitation

Imagine that you have been invited for a day out with your favourite character from a book.

- Write a letter of acceptance to your character.

To the helper:
- Talk about the character your child chooses and where the day out could be. Help with setting out the letter and with some of the writing. Remember to:
  - include the address, date, and so on;
  - thank for the invitation;
  - confirm the offer, time and meeting place;
  - express excitement and surprise at the invitation.

- Read the letter together.

Letter writing is an important skill which will be valuable in many areas of life.

_____ and
child

_____
helper(s)

_____

did this activity together

Holiday activities

To the helper:

● Discuss with your child what you are going to buy. If they are getting stuck on a word, help them by sounding it out.

This activity encourages children to attempt unknown spellings, an important step in learning to spell.

_____ and
child

_____
helper(s)

did this activity together

40 Holiday activities

Shopping spree

Ask your helper what you are going to eat today. What does your helper need to buy from the shops?

● Write a shopping list on this notepad.

Try and spell all the words yourself. How could you sort the things on your list?

impact WRITING HOMEWORK

Picture book present

Do you know somebody younger than you who likes new stories?

- Make a book for your friend by writing a story.
- Copy it out, a sentence on each page and draw a picture to go with each sentence.
- Put all the pages together and design a cover.
- Give it to the younger child.

To the helper:

- Look at some picture books and discuss the stories together. Suggest ideas for a simple story.
- Help to break the story down into single ideas and help with the spellings.

This activity encourages creative writing and develops ideas of the structure of a book.

_____ and
child

_____
helper(s)

_____
did this activity together

impact WRITING HOMEWORK

Holiday activities 41

To the helper:

- This would be a good follow-up to a trip to a museum.
- Help your child choose the exhibits and decide together what they could write. Accurate spelling is not important, in this case.
- Visit their museum!

This activity enables children to see that different styles of writing are used in different contexts.

_____ and

child

_____

helper(s)

_____

did this activity together

Model museum

- Make your own museum! It could be:
  - a toy museum
  - a LEGO land
  - a natural history museum (use your stuffed toys)
  - a car museum.

- Choose a few exhibits. Write a label with a small description of each thing.

- Design a poster to encourage your family or friends to come to your museum.

Illuminated room sign

In the Middle Ages there weren't any computers and printers so the monks had to copy out books by hand. They used to do the first letter larger and decorate it like this:

This is called an 'illuminated letter'.

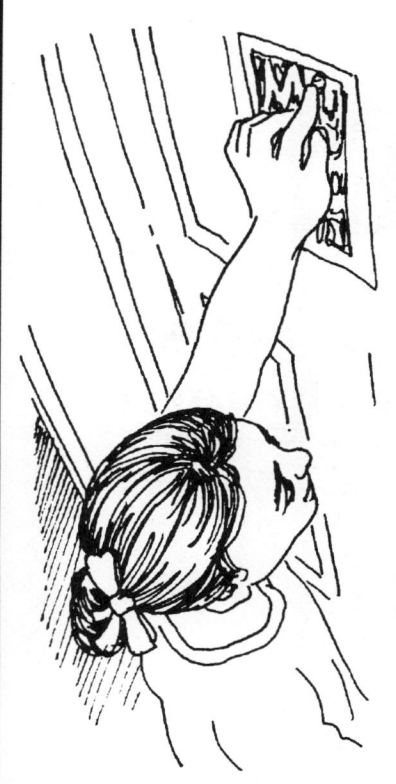

- Design a sign for your bedroom door with an illuminated letter.

To the helper:

- Encourage your child to practice in rough first and then to produce a finished design which can be coloured in.

The ability to produce different styles of handwriting is important.

_____ and
child

_____
helper(s)

_____
did this activity together

Holiday activities

To the helper:

● Start the activity with the children finding their names. Extend the scope by choosing other words or names to find. For these other categories the words can be graded for different aged players.

This activity reinforces spellings of common words.

_____ and
child

_____
helper(s)

did this activity together

44   Holiday activities

Number plate names

When you go on a journey in a car look out of the car window at the number plates.

● See if you can spot the letters of your name in order (grown ups have to use both names).

Shout out each letter when you see it. The first to finish their name wins.

Now try it with everyone having a different fruit, animal, vegetable or country name to find.

'E', I have an 'E' in my name!

impact WRITING HOMEWORK

Going away

If you are going away on holiday what are you leaving behind?

It might be a pet, a plant or a favourite toy.

- Write instructions for someone to look after whatever it is while you're away.

To the helper:

- Ask your child to think about what needs to be done for the item.
- Help them to write it clearly, taking account of other perspectives. Help them with the spelling.

This activity enables children to see a purpose for writing. It develops their ability to produce instructional writing.

_____and

child

_____

helper(s)

_____

did this activity together

Holiday activities

To the helper:

- Decide on the range of ingredients you want your child to use.
- Discuss suitable names – look at menus or food packets when you're in the shops – help them with spellings in their descriptions. Help your child make exactly what they have written.

This activity demonstrates to children how different styles of writing are used in different contexts. It gives writing a purpose.

_____and

child

_____

helper(s)

_____

did this activity together

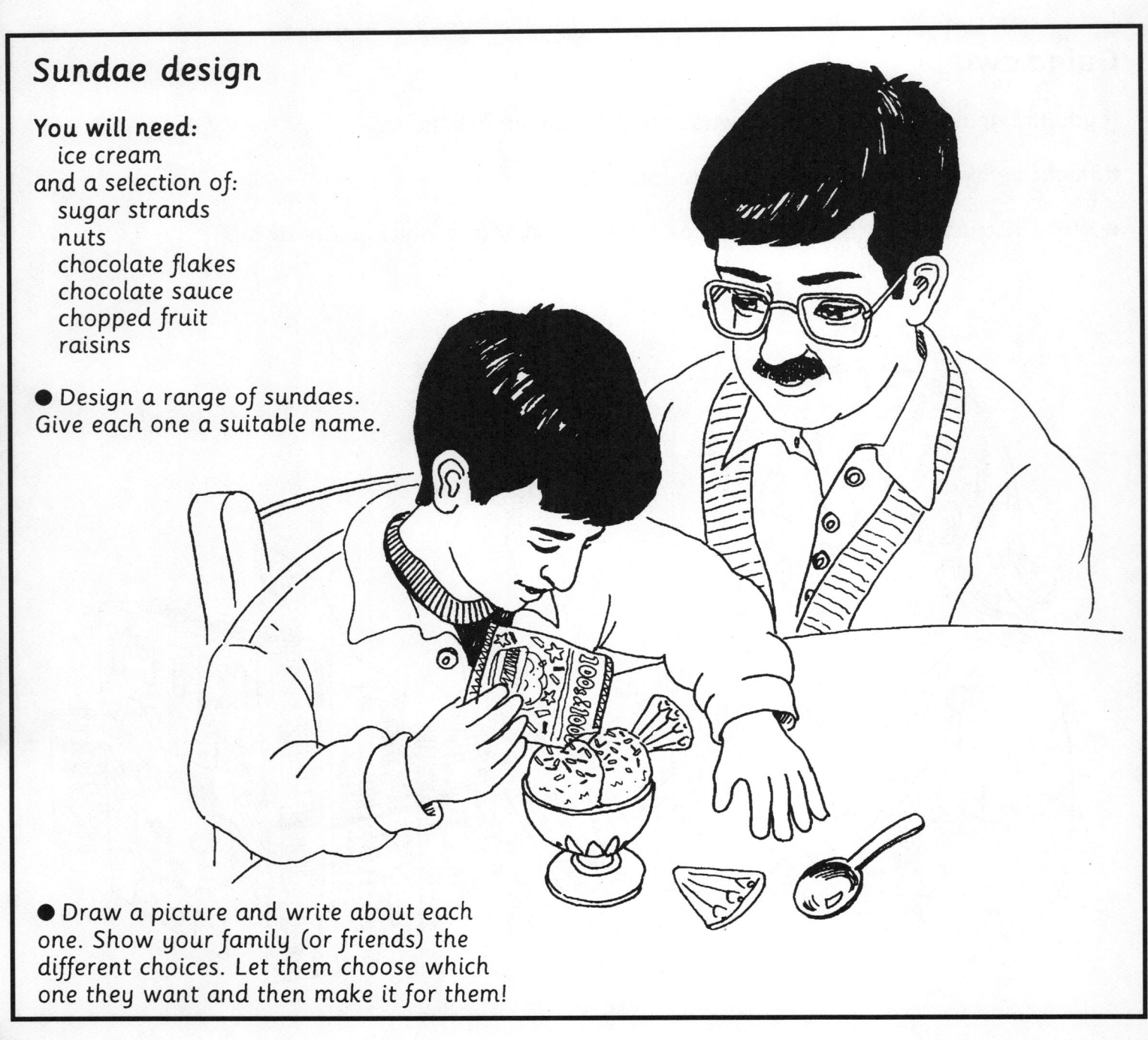

Sundae design

You will need:
ice cream
and a selection of:
sugar strands
nuts
chocolate flakes
chocolate sauce
chopped fruit
raisins

- Design a range of sundaes. Give each one a suitable name.

- Draw a picture and write about each one. Show your family (or friends) the different choices. Let them choose which one they want and then make it for them!

Fan letter

- Look at all your books. Which is your favourite one? Why do you like it?

- Find out the name of the author and write them a letter, telling them why you like their book.

To the helper:
- Brainstorm with your child what it is they like about the book.
- Help them set out a letter, using the correct format. Make sure they include their address for a reply.
- Send the letter to the author, care of the publishers.

This activity encourages book-review skills. It teaches the children how letters should be set out. It also demonstrates a purpose of writing.

_____and

child

_____

helper(s)

_____

did this activity together

impact WRITING HOMEWORK

Holiday activities

To the helper:

- Please help by having two lists on paper. One titled 'th' as in thumb and the other 'th' as in the.
- Make a list of about five words on each piece of paper. Read the words together.
- You may like to write sentences using a word from each list.

These two letters make two sounds depending on the other letters in the word.

_____ and

child

_____

helper(s)

_____

did this activity together

Holiday activities

Make two lists

How many words can you think of that have the letters 'th' in them?

- Sort them into two lists: one list where your tongue goes between your teeth (like **th**ing, **Th**ursday, fil**th**y) and another where your tongue strokes the back of your teeth (**th**ose, **th**at, bro**th**er).

impact WRITING HOMEWORK

second oo sound

1. Fill in the missing letters and say the finished words.

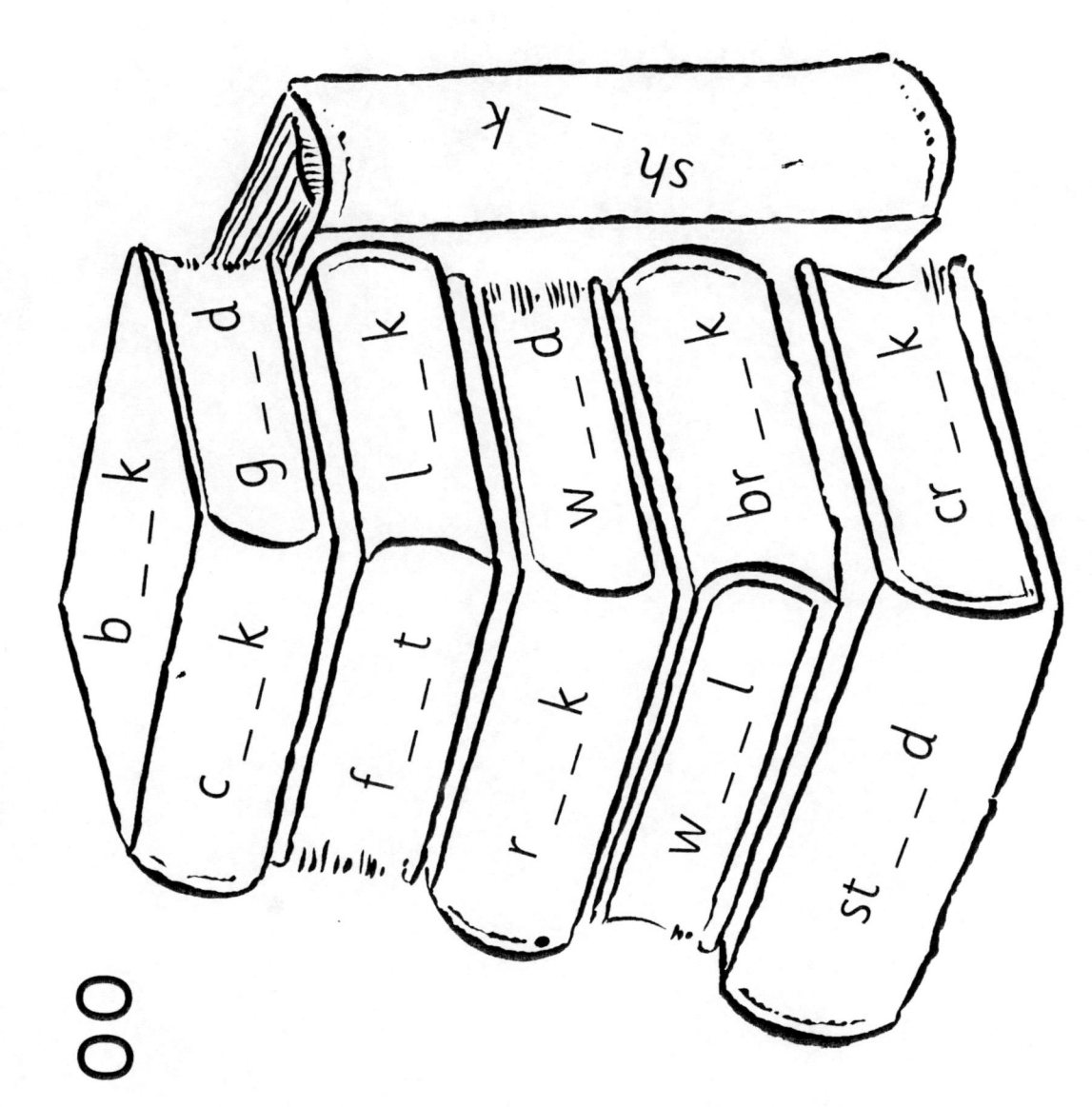

oo

b _ _ k, c _ _ k, d _ _ g _ _ k, l _ _ k, f _ _ t, r _ _ k, w _ _ d, w _ _ l, br _ _ k, cr _ _ k, st _ _ d, sh _ _ k

2. Write the words you have made.

3. Write three more words with the same sound in them.

first **oo** sound

1. Fill in the missing letters and say the finished words.

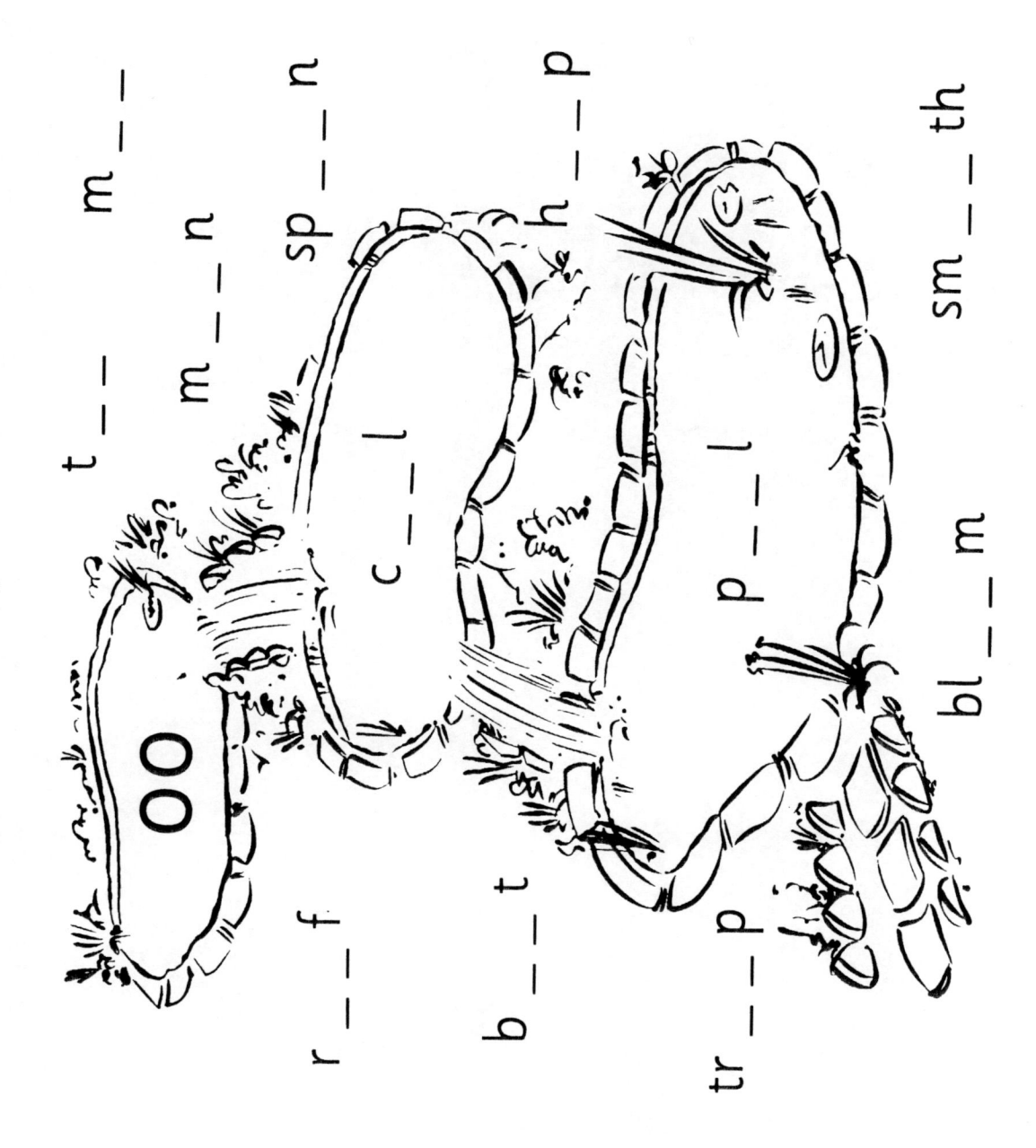

r _ _ f
t _ _ m _ _
b _ _ t
m _ _ n
c _ _ l
sp _ _ n
tr _ _ p
p _ _ l
h _ _ p
bl _ _ m
sm _ _ th

2. Write the words you have made.

3. Write three more words with the same sound in them.

Draw a map

● Draw your own map to show the journey you will take to go on holiday or for a day out.

You will need a map to help you.

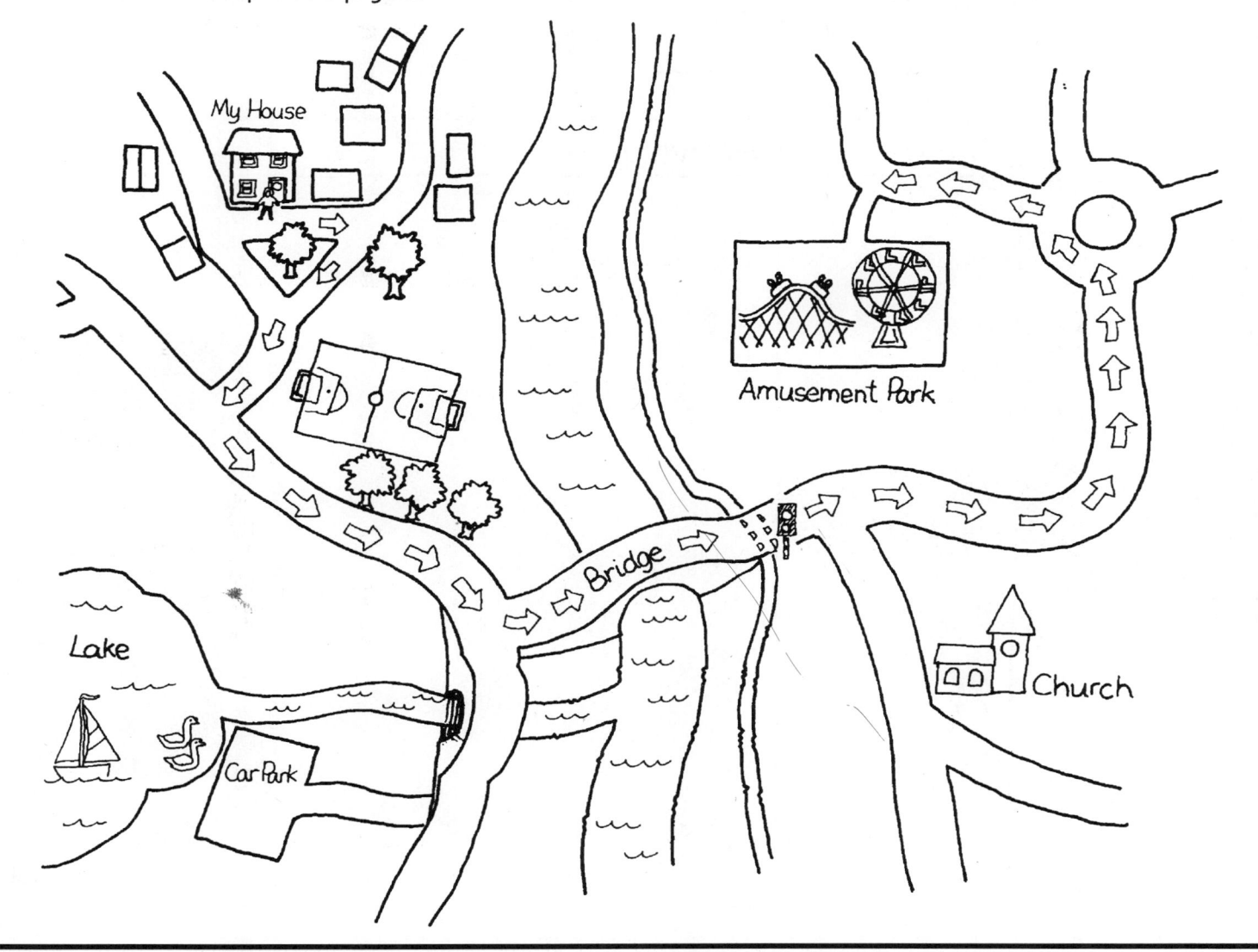

(Map showing: My House, Amusement Park, Bridge, Lake, Car Park, Church)

impact WRITING HOMEWORK

To the helper:

- Help your child to find your home town and your holiday destination on a map of the UK.
- Talk through your route and look out for:
- towns that you will by pass;
- motorways or roads taken;
- whether it is a long or short journey.

This is an ideal activity before your holiday. Your child will then be able to help with the navigation by responding to the destination road signs. This activity will also help your child to begin to become familiar with maps.

_____and
child

_____
helper(s)

_____
did this activity together

Holiday activities   49

To the helper:

- Take time to discuss the day's activities together.
- It may help to have three sheets of paper labelled, morning, afternoon and evening.

Planning is essential in life. This activity will help your child to be systematic and to plan logically.

_____ and
child

_____
helper(s)

_____
did this activity together

Holiday activities

Make a timetable

How are you going to spend your day?

- Make up a timetable to show what you are going to do for a day. It can be real or made up!

Day _____

Time	Activity

impact WRITING HOMEWORK

My favourite sports kit

- Draw a picture of yourself wearing a sports kit which you would like to own.

- Label your drawing.

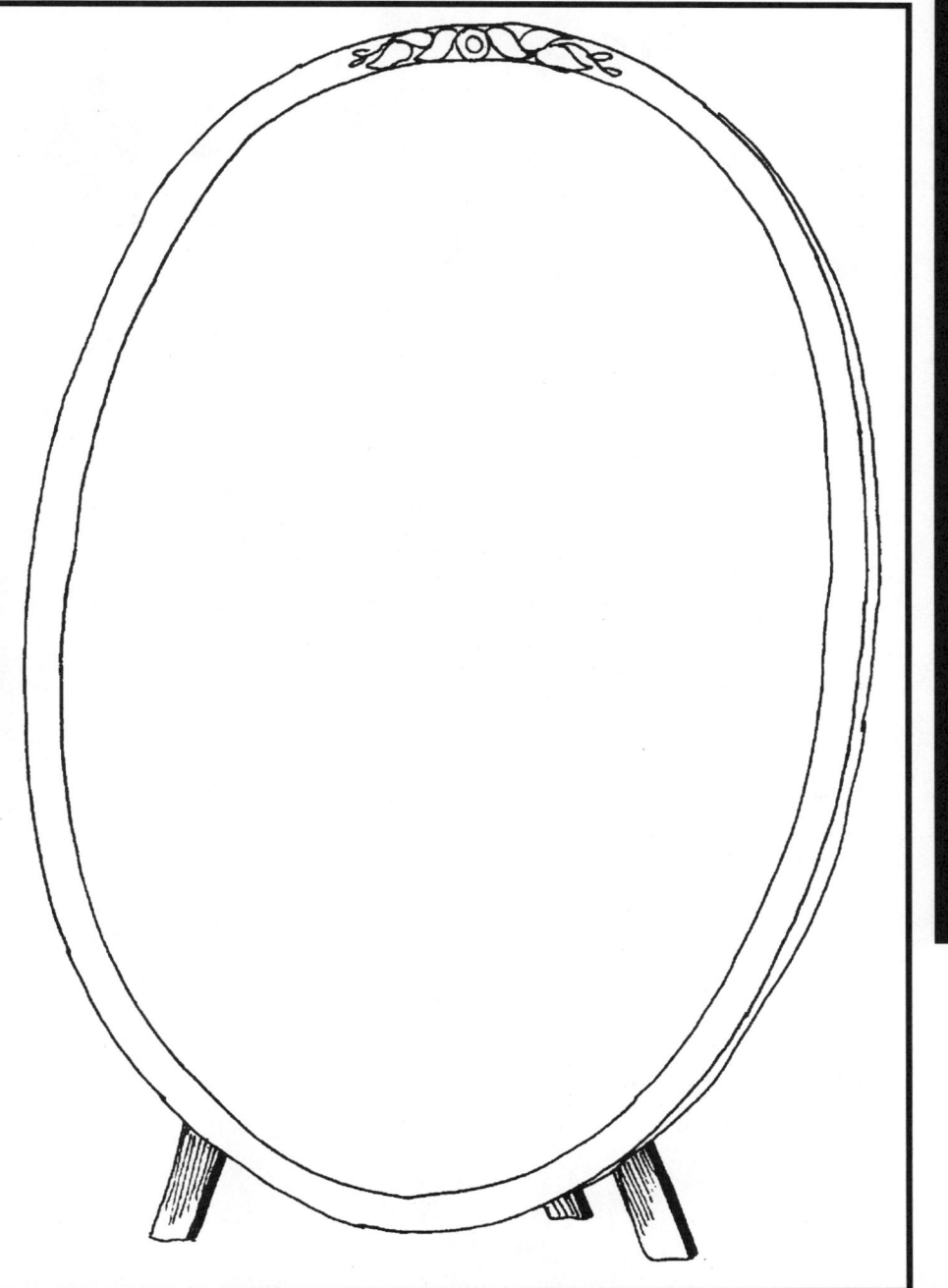

To the helper:

- You may like to look in magazines, newspapers or books to give you ideas.
- Ask your child to write the labels on to separate pieces of paper to read before copying onto the picture.
- Encourage your child to write a sentence to describe each article of clothing if he/she is keen to do so. Remind your child that sentences always begin with a capital letter and end with a full stop.

Writing about topics which interest them helps children develop spelling, puncutation and descriptive writing skills.

_____ and
child

_____
helper(s)

_____
did this activity together

impact WRITING HOMEWORK   Holiday activities   51

To the helper:

- First brainstorm some verbs. Say them together. Keep the verbs in the present tense (as though they were doing it *now*). It may help to write them down.
- Don't point the pattern out to the child, they will learn better if they spot it themselves!

This activity makes explicit the usual conjugation of the present tense we use in English. It will help in their writing and in learning a foreign language later.

_____and
child

_____
helper(s)

_____
did this activity together

52   Holiday activities

Change a verb

A verb is a doing word. It has a different ending, depending on who is doing it.

For example **to sing**

I sing
You sing
He sings
She sings
They sing

- Think of some more verbs. Say them to yourself. How do they change depending on who does it.

Can you spot any patterns or rules?

Are there any verbs which do not fit the pattern?

impact WRITING HOMEWORK

Invent a word

You can make new words by putting two words together.

playground
blackberry
football

● Make up some of your own words and draw pictures to show what they mean!

For example:
legbands or foamspray

To the helper:

● If you can't think of any new words start with an existing compound word and just change one of the words for example: wristwatch – anklewatch.

This activity shows children how the English language is changing all the time and how new words may be developed.

_____ and
child

_____
helper(s)

_____
did this activity together

impact WRITING HOMEWORK

Holiday activities 53

To the helper:

● This game is best played between children of similar abilities.

The activity helps children become aware of common letter patterns in spelling. It also gives them dictionary practice.

_____and
child

_____
helper(s)

_____

did this activity together

54 **Holiday activities**

Alphabet soup

● Choose one of your reading books, close your eyes and point to seven different letters in turn. Write them down.

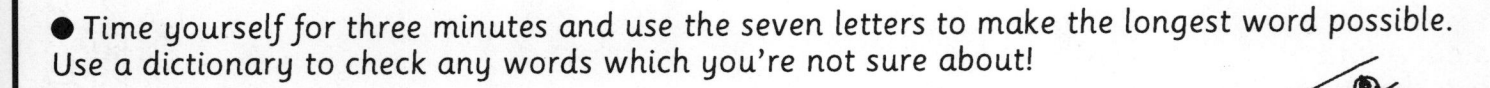

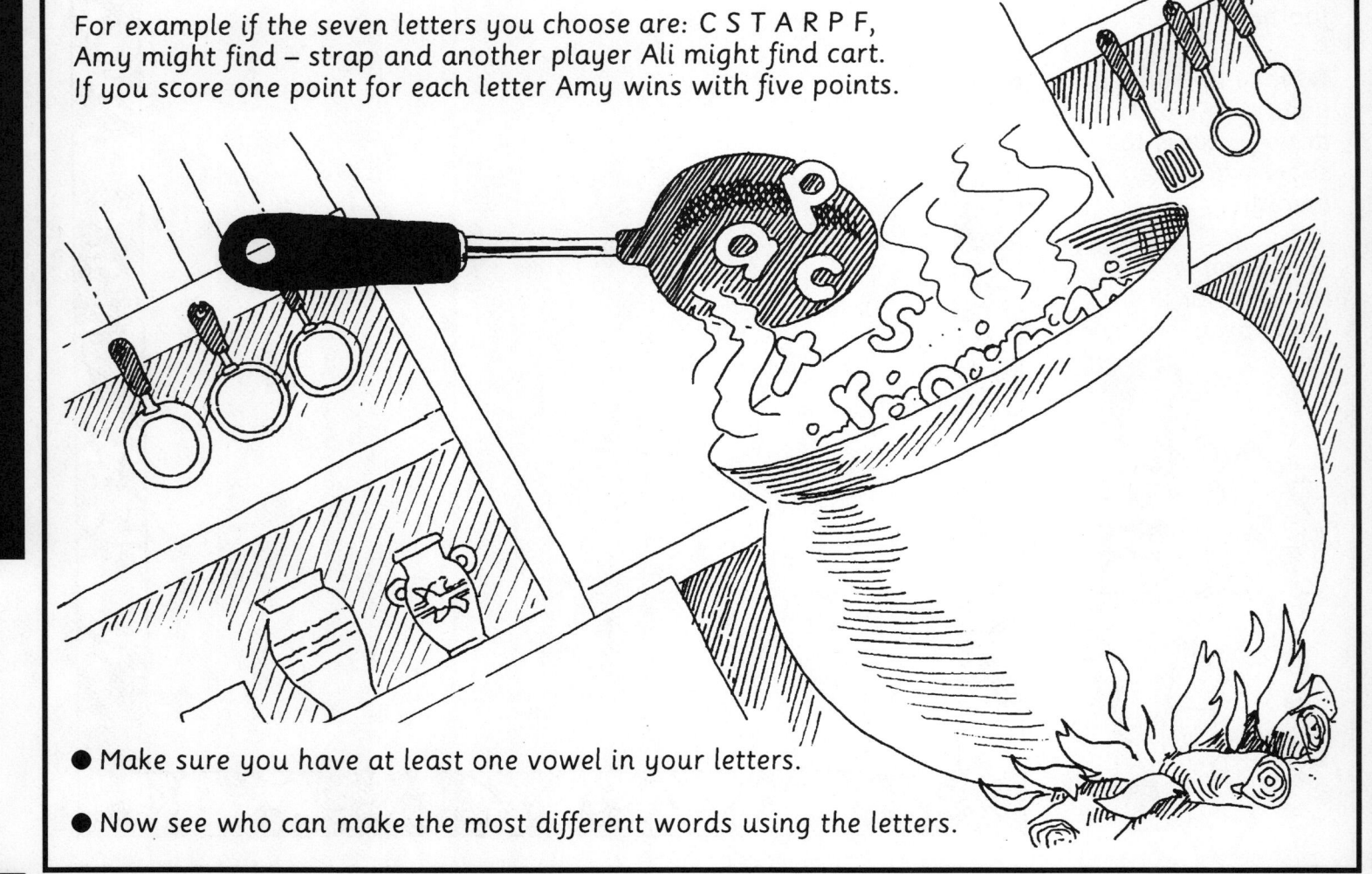

● Time yourself for three minutes and use the seven letters to make the longest word possible. Use a dictionary to check any words which you're not sure about!

For example if the seven letters you choose are: C S T A R P F,
Amy might find – strap and another player Ali might find cart.
If you score one point for each letter Amy wins with five points.

● Make sure you have at least one vowel in your letters.

● Now see who can make the most different words using the letters.

impact **WRITING HOMEWORK**

Design a card

- Make a card for a friend or relation.

- Design a picture for the cover and write a poem to go inside.

You could do an acrostic:

> Grey hair
> Really cuddly
> Always kind
> Never shouts
> Nearly always smiling
> You're great

A list poem:

> I love you Granny because...
> You're funny and you're cuddly
> You're kind and you're generous
> You play nice games
> You're completely marvellous.

Or you could write another sort of poem.

To the helper:

- Let the child decide the sort of poem they want to write. Brainstorm ideas about the person.
- Help with writing the poem, check spellings and maybe improve the way it scans.
- Encourage them to write it up in their best writing. Discuss what sort of picture to put on the cover.

Learning to read and write syllables gives children confidence in spelling and is a helpful strategy for identifying words.

_____and

child

_____

helper(s)

_____

did this activity together

Holiday activities

To the helper:

- You may want to brainstorm some ideas of places where a clue could be hidden.
- Encourage your child to try writing the clues and then go through them together to check they are clear. Help them to simplify them for younger children.

The clues rely on rhymes, synonyms, homonyms and plays on words – all of these help children gain a better awareness of language in its written form.

_____ and
child

_____
helper(s)

_____
did this activity together

Treasure hunt

- Plan a treasure hunt for your friends. Give them a clue to somewhere at home. Hide another clue at that place, sending them somewhere else and so on...

- Hide some 'treasure' at the last place.

Clues could be like these:

| Go up them | Fill in the blanks: |
| Rhymes with chairs | do ti la __ __ me re do |

- Think of who is going to do the treasure hunt, and make the clues more difficult if you need to!

56 Holiday activities

impact WRITING HOMEWORK

What's cooking?

Who does the cooking in your home?

- Ask them to help you plan a meal that you can make together.

- Design a menu for the meal. Include descriptions of each dish, try to use as many describing words as you can.

Menu

To the helper:

- You may want to look at menus beforehand (menus for pizza delivery often come through the door) to spot the sort of language they use and how the writing is set out.

This should give the children practice in descriptive writing.

_____ and
child

_____
helper(s)

did this activity together

impact WRITING HOMEWORK

Holiday activities 57

To the helper:

● When you pick words, try and make sure the consonants and vowels are in the same position in the word: head – tail is much easier than head – knee.

This activity encourages awareness of common letter patterns in spelling.

_____and
child

_____
helper(s)

_____
did this activity together

Holiday activities

Change a letter

● Think of two words with the same number of letters.

For example:
CAT
DOG

● Change one letter at a time, so it still makes a word, until you get to the other word:
CAT
COT
COG
DOG

● See who can do it in the fewest steps:
MAN
MAD
BAD
BAY
BOY

MAN
MAY
BAY
BOY

impact WRITING HOMEWORK

Alphabet race

- When you next go on a car journey, play this game.

- Divide everyone in your car into two teams (the people sitting on the right are one team, the people on the left the other). The game is to collect all the letters of the alphabet, in order from A to Z from road signs, shop names, adverts or anywhere you can see words. The team on the left can only use words on the left-hand side of the car and the team on the right can only use words on the right. Each sign can only be used to gain one letter. For example:

You can use the 'a' from Bay as your first letter, but you will need to wait for another sign to collect your 'b'.

The first team to Z wins – good luck!

a	b	c	d	e	f	g	h	i	j	k	l	m
n	o	p	q	r	s	t	u	v	w	x	y	z

a	b	c	d	e	f	g	h	i	j	k	l	m
n	o	p	q	r	s	t	u	v	w	x	y	z

To the helper:

- Help your child to look for their letters and keep track of what letters they need next.
- Talk about what letters are easy to 'find' and which ones are hard.

This game will help reinforce alphabetical order and give you a chance to look at letter frequency within words. You can also look at the formation of words and letter use.

_____and
child

_____
helper(s)

_____

did this activity together

impact WRITING HOMEWORK

Holiday activities

To the helper:

- You may have to help the children reading some unusual names.
- Discuss any meanings they don't know for example – The Nelson.
- You may have to act as Umpire in difficult situations for example – The Coach and Horses.

This activity encourages children to read for meaning.

_____and

child

_____

helper(s)

_____

did this activity together

Pub bingo

- Divide the people in your car into two teams. One team takes the left-hand side of the road, the other takes the right.

- Look out for pub signs on your side of the road. Score one point for each 'leg' in your pub name.

For example:
The White Horse   scores 4
The Eagle and Child   scores 4
The Rat and Carrot   scores 4
The Slug and Lettuce   scores 0

The winning team is the one with the most points at the end of the journey!

Holiday activities

impact WRITING HOMEWORK

Strong and weak verbs

There are two sorts of verbs (doing words) in English.

There are weak verbs, which you put into the past by adding – ed.

And there are strong verbs which change their vowel sound in the past.

● Make a list here of strong verbs in the present tense and then write down what they change to in the past tense. The list has been started for you, now think of some more.

Present (now)
run
sing

Past (already done)
ran
sang

To the helper:

● Brainstorm a list of 'doing' words. Talk about how they change in the past tense. Write down the 'strong' ones.

This activity forms part of the work on tenses we will be doing back in class. It is important to draw children's attention to irregular verb forms as they often over-generalise the 'add –ed' rule.

_____and
child

_____
helper(s)

_____

did this activity together

Holiday activities

To the helper:

- Look through gardening books or books about plants with your child.
- Help them to answer the questions and encourage them to be as original as possible.
- A trip to a garden centre or greenhouse would add interest to the activity.

There is a 'specialist' vocabulary for gardening and this activity will help children explore and widen their understanding.

_____and
child

_____
helper(s)

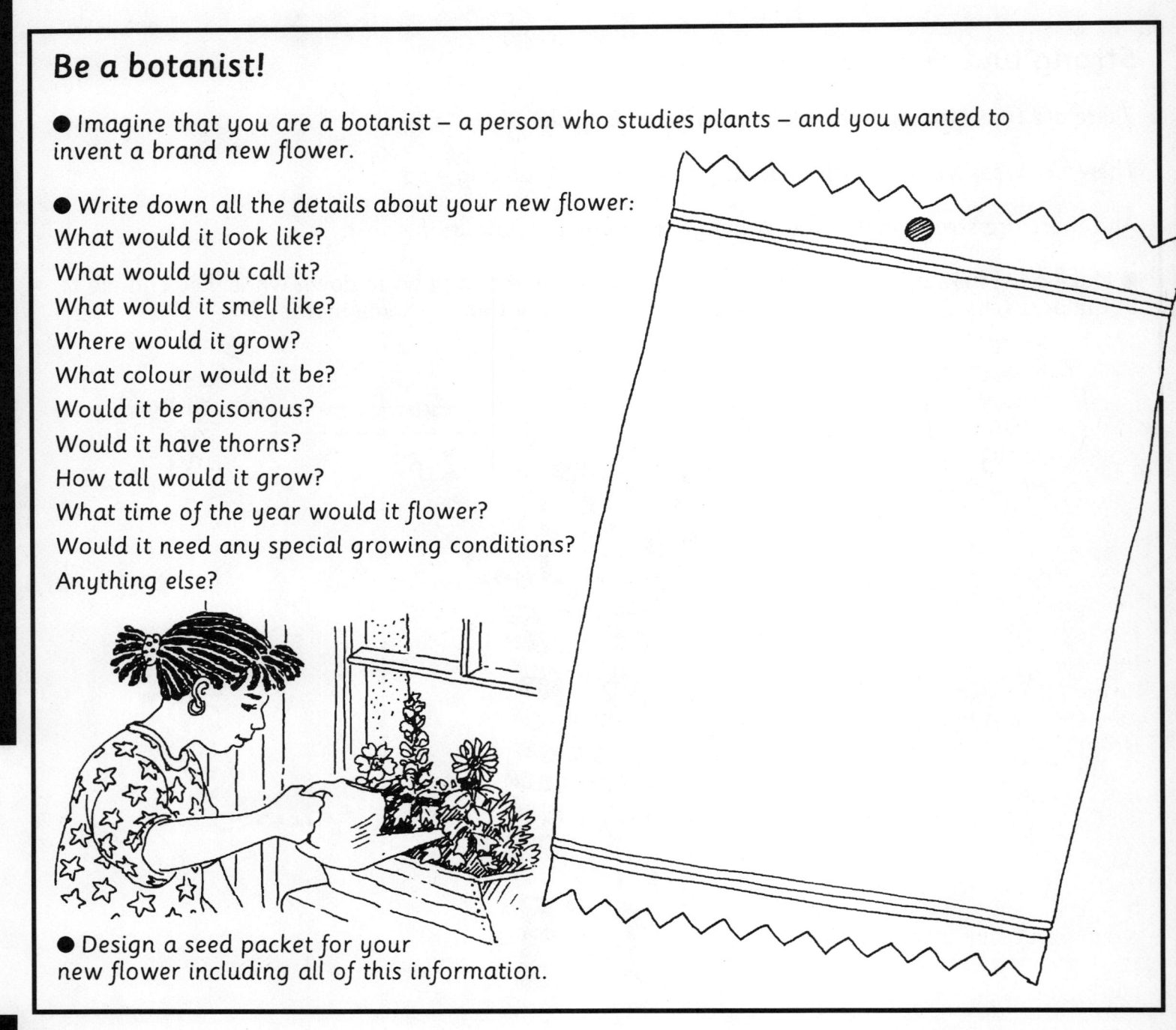

_____
did this activity together

Be a botanist!

- Imagine that you are a botanist – a person who studies plants – and you wanted to invent a brand new flower.

- Write down all the details about your new flower:

What would it look like?
What would you call it?
What would it smell like?
Where would it grow?
What colour would it be?
Would it be poisonous?
Would it have thorns?
How tall would it grow?
What time of the year would it flower?
Would it need any special growing conditions?
Anything else?

- Design a seed packet for your new flower including all of this information.

62 **Holiday activities**

impact WRITING HOMEWORK

Word chains

- Play this game with a group of people.

- Sit in a circle, or decide what order turns you will take (you could even play in the car).

- Choose a topic (animals, countries, items of clothing) and a person to start the game.

This is how you play:

The first person thinks of a word within the category, such as 'lion'.

The next person needs to think of a word that begins with the last letter of this word, for example 'newt' (from the 'n' in 'lion').

Play continues until someone can't think of a suitable word. They are then out. Play carries on until there is only one person left, who is the winner and can choose what category to play next! Words may not be repeated within a round.

To the helper:

- If you get bogged down by a particular letter (if all the words end in 'e' for example), you can choose to use the second to last letter.
- You may want to impose a time limit to each person's turn or give everyone access to a dictionary.

This game will help reinforce initial and final letter sounds. It is an excellent chance to widen children's vocabulary within certain subject areas.

_____and

child

_____

helper(s)

_____

did this activity together

Holiday activities

To the helper:

- Look at some brochures first, so the child gets some idea of the writing style and what information they contain.
- Encourage them to rewrite information in leaflets of their own.
- Make sure they plan and organise the work before doing it. This is best carried out while the information is fresh in their minds.

This activity shows writing for a purpose. It can also provide an interesting record of a holiday for years to come.

_____and
child

_____
helper(s)

_____

did this activity together

Make a scrapbook

● While you are on holiday take photos and collect leaflets about the places you go and the things you see.

● Design a scrapbook about the place to tell people:

- what there is to do
- what the place is like
- where the place is
- what the accommodation is like
- about people they may meet

● Make your language enthusiastic and descriptive to encourage people to go.

● If you're not going away, make up a fantasy brochure – a holiday on the moon, maybe?

What will you do tomorrow?

When you talk about something you are **going** to do it is called the future tense.

- Make a list of all the ways you could say you will play tomorrow.

For example:

I am going to play tomorrow
I will play tomorrow

To the helper:

- Brainstorm the ways the children talk about what they are going to do tomorrow. Suggest that they ask friends and family as there are often individual differences in the way people speak.

This activity will draw children's attention to the various forms of the future tense in the English language. Back in school we will discuss variation in meaning.

_____ and
child

_____
helper(s)

_____
did this activity together

Holiday activities

To the helper:

- Brainstorm the ways the children can think of to say it rained yesterday. Suggest that they ask friends and family as there are often individual differences in the way people speak.
- Help them with the spelling.

This work will bring the children's attention to the various forms of the past tense in the English language. Back in class we will be discussing the variation in meaning.

_____ and
child

_____
helper(s)

_____
did this activity together

What happened yesterday?

There are lots of ways of talking about things that have already happened. We call this the past tense.

● Think of as many ways as you can to say it rained yesterday.

For example:

It had rained yesterday
It rained yesterday

66   Holiday activities

impact WRITING HOMEWORK

Bored games?

Have you run out of games to play? Why don't you design your own?
- Plan it in rough and then make a final version. (Use a cereal packet to make a board.)
- Make all the pieces and a box for it.
- Write the instructions and stick them on the box.
- Play your game with a friend.

To the helper:
- If your child is stuck for ideas suggest they take a game they like and just design a new version.
- Play the rough version together and work on improvements together. You may have to help them with the rules – look at existing games rules for ideas.
- Help them to think of ways they could change their language if the meaning is not clear.

Writing instructions is an important form of writing to master. To be successful children have to take other people's points of view and be unambiguous in their use of language.

_____and
child

_____
helper(s)

_____
did this activity together

impact WRITING HOMEWORK

Holiday activities 67

To the helper:

- Encourage players to draw quickly without adding too much detail. You may have to play a few games to get the hang of it.
- Spelling isn't important but speed and secrecy are!

Children will become more precise at using language to describe the pictures. It shows how meanings change and get distorted over time. It's also great fun!

_____and

child

_____

helper(s)

_____

did this activity together

Words and pictures

- Try this game with some other members of your family. Each person needs a piece of paper and a pen and you should sit in a circle.

- Everyone writes a sentence at the top of their paper and then passes it on to the next person. You mustn't let anyone else see what you have written.

- When you get your second piece of paper draw a quick sketch of what is written. Fold over the sentence so only the picture can be seen and pass it on again.

- Look at the picture you have received and write a sentence to describe it and pass it on (folding over the picture first).

The game continues until everyone has had a go, or you run out of paper!

- Open it up and see how the meaning has changed:

The cow jumped over the moon
The cow jumped over the moon
Pigs might fly

Foreign dictionary

If you are going on holiday to a country where they speak another language, why not make a dictionary.

- Find out different words in the language and what they mean.
- Draw a picture for each one.

Decide how you are going to arrange your words – in topics (such as food, clothes or greetings.) in alphabetical order or another way.

To the helper:
- Start off with a list of words and then arrange them.
- Look around for more words such as on food wrappers in the supermarket or on signs.
- Perhaps your child could use a phrase book.
- If the child decides to make the book alphabetical, are they going to use the English or other language, or both?

This activity raises awareness of other languages. It may also show any common roots between English and another language. It will give a useful insight into different types of dictionaries.

_____and
child

_____
helper(s)

_____
did this activity together

Holiday activities

To the helper:

- You may want to select number plates which have easy letter combinations (not with X, Z or Q).
- If the child is having difficulty start them off with one of the words.

This activity helps children with initial letter sounds. It also provides a useful mnemonic strategy for them to use when they are older.

_____ and

child

_____

helper(s)

_____

did this activity together

Holiday activities

Number plate phrase

Next time you're out in the car try this word game.

- Look at the car in front's number plate.
- Make up a phrase using the three-letter part as initial letters.

For example:

D247 GRF Going Really Fast!

Write a play

- Get together with a group of friends or your brothers and sisters. Choose a story to make into a script for a play, or write your own. Write down what everyone is going to say – try and tell the whole story just by people speaking.

- Perform your play to your parents, big brothers and sisters or friends.

You could design programmes for the audience or posters to advertise the play.

To the helper:

- You may want to help the children pick a story that will be easy to turn into a play.
- If they are stuck for what to write, suggest they practise it first and write down what people say.
- Encourage them to redraft to make improvements.

The ability to write a script is an important form of writing to practise. It should help them make dialogue realistic, which will help in story writing.

_____and
child

_____
helper(s)

_____

did this activity together

Holiday activities

To the helper:

- Brainstorm what the child wants to say first.
- Help them with the standard format for a letter.
- Encourage them to find the addresses for themselves. Make sure you enclose your own address for a reply.

Children should be aware of standard conventions of letter writing. This activity will give them practice in this and also provide a purpose for writing.

_____ and
child

_____
helper(s)

did this activity together

What's on TV?

What's your favourite programme?

What do you like about it?

What don't you like about it?

Is it still on TV, is it being repeated?

- Write a letter to the television company that shows the programme telling them your views.

Television companies rely on viewer feedback to decide on their programme schedules.

Time capsule

We can find out a lot about life in the past from artefacts.

- Make a collection of artefacts that would tell someone about your life now.

- Write a bit about yourself – include your name, age, what you look like, what you like eating, what you like doing and something about your family.

- Put the things in a plastic box and bury it in the garden.

You could mark the spot and write instructions on when it should be dug up or you could leave it to chance!

To the helper:
- Discuss with your child what might be interesting to people in the future.
- Discuss what would be suitable to put in the box.

This activity should encourage children to plan their work. It encourages them to write descriptively within a purposeful framework.

_____ and
child

_____
helper(s)

_____

did this activity together

impact WRITING HOMEWORK

Holiday activities

To the helper:

- Help your child identify four characters and the setting (where the story takes place).
- Look through the book together identifying all the adjectives related to your chosen words. Add the words to webs as illustrated.
- As you find the adjectives, talk with your child about where they are within the sentence and how they are formed.

Adjectives add depth and meaning to writing. It is important to be able to identify adjectives in context and understand their placement and formation.

_____ and
child

_____
helper(s)

_____
did this activity together

Adjective hunt

- Look through your reading book or any book that you may have at home that you have read and enjoyed. Pick out the four main characters and the main place of action.

- Look through the book and find as many adjectives (describing words) as you can that describe your chosen nouns (people, places or things).

- Write them in web form like this:

```
     green      fierce
       ↖        ↗
scaly ← dragon → agile
       ↙        ↘
     greedy     angry
```

- Talk with your helper about the different adjectives used. Now write a brief description for each character and place, using the words you have found.

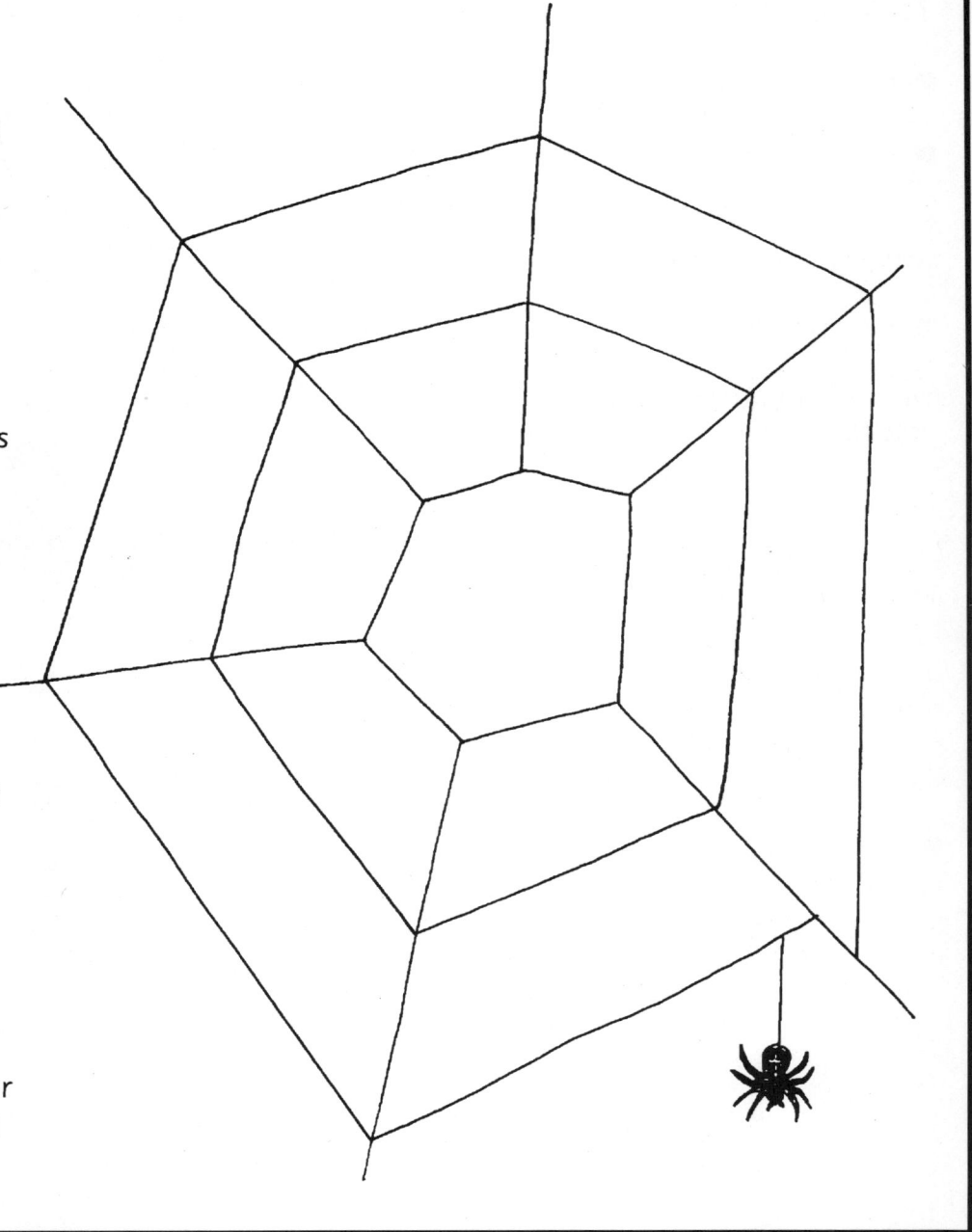

74 **Holiday activities**

Thanks a lot!

- Imagine that you have just received a gift from your Aunt Floribunda. As usual she has given you a very interesting gift, but you really don't like it. How can you thank Aunt Floribunda without hurting her feelings?

- Talk with your helper about the best way to write a thank you letter for a gift you don't like.

- Think of an imaginary awful gift and write a letter of thanks.

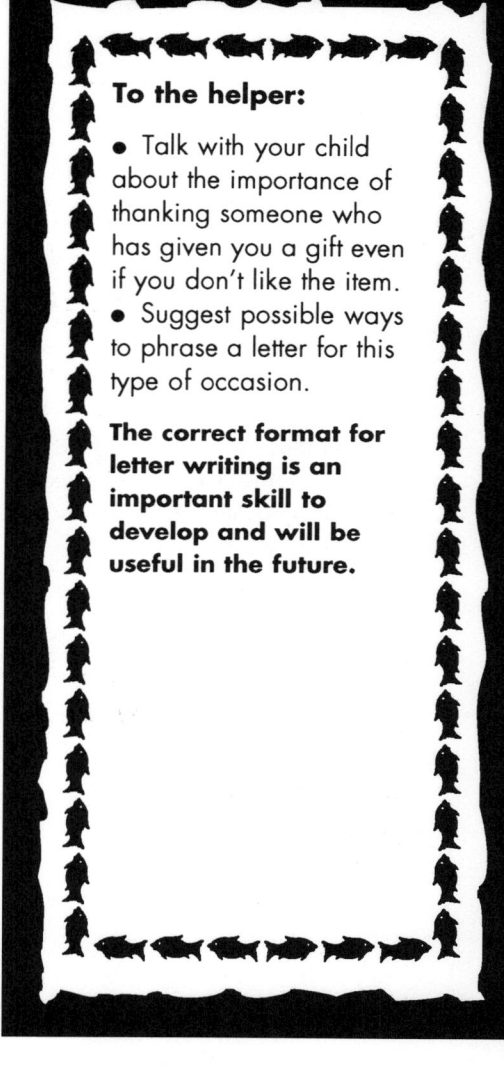

To the helper:

- Talk with your child about the importance of thanking someone who has given you a gift even if you don't like the item.
- Suggest possible ways to phrase a letter for this type of occasion.

The correct format for letter writing is an important skill to develop and will be useful in the future.

_____ and
child

_____
helper(s)

_____

did this activity together

impact WRITING HOMEWORK

Holiday activities

To the helper:

- This game can be played anywhere, by any number of people. You could ask the players to add sentences instead of words if you choose, but single words make the story more random.
- Everyone will have to think on their feet and help each other out if someone gets stuck!

This activity focuses attention on story structure and word use. It also encourages quick thinking and can be useful in vocabulary development.

_____and

child

_____

helper(s)

_____

did this activity together

Holiday activities

One at a time

You will need a group of friends to play this game. You are going to create a new story together.

● Take it in turns and one at a time add a word to the story. Each person adds a new word – it must fit with the story and make sense with the word which the last person has said.

One...day...a...boy...named...Abraham...went...to...the...moon...on...the...space...shuttle.

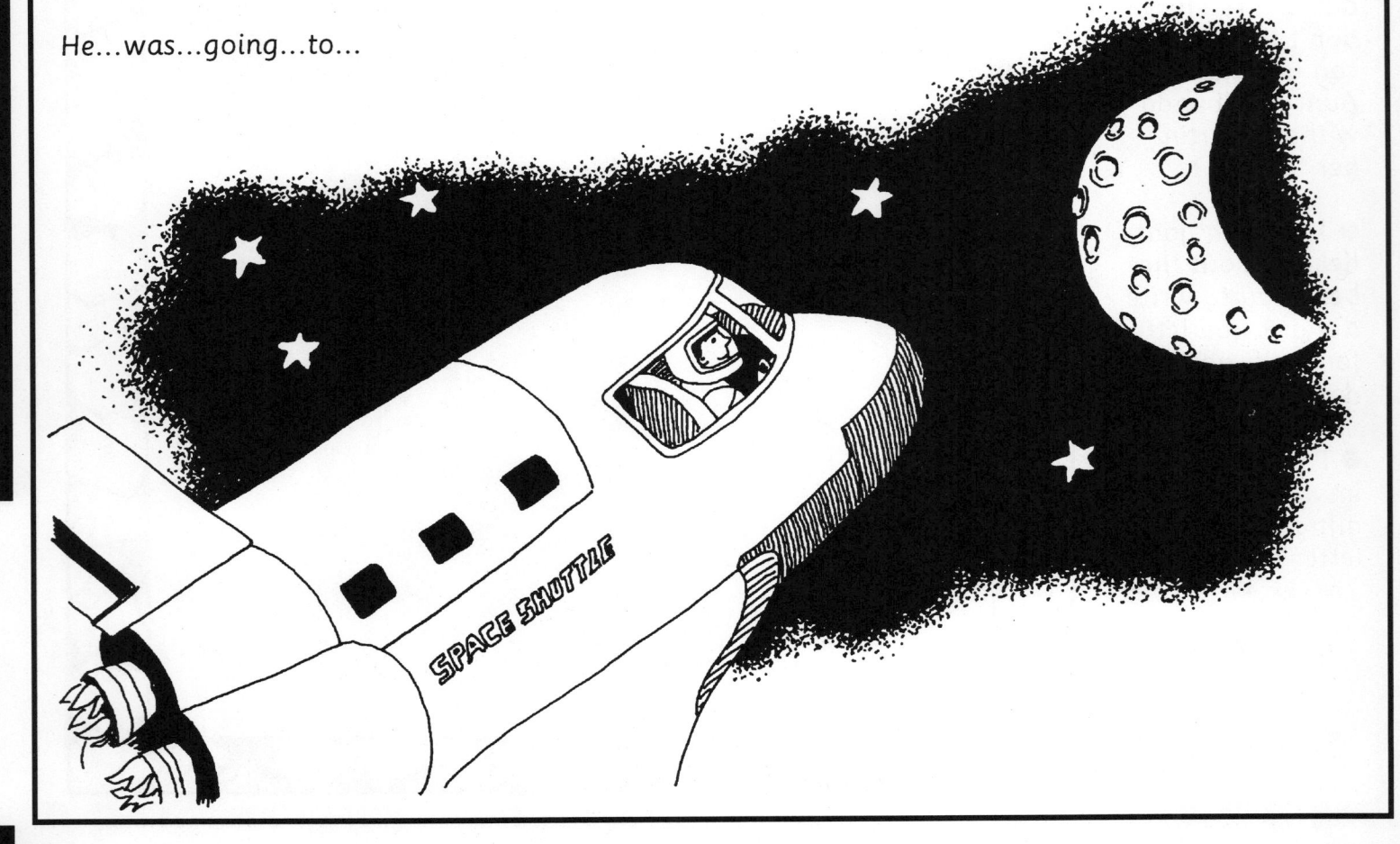

He...was...going...to...

impact WRITING HOMEWORK

Brilliant barbecue

● Imagine that you have invited four of your best friends over for a barbecue. Of course, you want the meal to be brilliant!

What will you serve first? Second? Next? What will you serve for dessert?

● Carefully plan a menu so that all the foods go well together.

● Write out the menu when you've chosen the food.

To the helper:

● Look through recipe books together to find dishes that sound tasty, easy to prepare and easy to clean up after!

● Encourage your child to write out the menu, making it sound appetising and look interesting.

It is important for children to think about how food is selected and presented for a meal. Looking through cookery books is an interesting activity in itself and can give rise to a variety of conversations about cooking and food terms.

_____and
child

_____
helper(s)

_____
did this activity together

impact WRITING HOMEWORK   Holiday activities

To the helper:

- Encourage your child to list five different things that describe their chosen person or thing.
- Remind your child that a new paragraph starts on a new line and is indented (spaced in) about five spaces to the right on the first line.

Paragraphs are important in the organisation of writing – both imaginative and factual. Children need to write in paragraphs to give their written work clarity. A focus on different attributes gives each paragraph a main idea and makes the writing process easier to understand.

_____ and
child

_____
helper(s)

_____

did this activity together

Five paragraphs

- Choose one of these:

Your best friend
Your favourite food
Your pet
(or anything of your choice)

- Make a list of five things that describe your chosen person, place or thing.

- Now use these five decriptions to write five different paragraphs about your chosen person, place or thing.

- Now use the five points to write five paragraphs (Don't forget to indent!)

Rachael is: funny, friendly, helpful, kind, thoughtful.

Rachael is my best friend. She is very funny. She tells great stories and knows lots of jokes. She can make anyone smile, even when they are quite sad. She told us a story about...

Rachael is incredibly friendly. She has many...

78 Holiday activities

impact WRITING HOMEWORK

Design a brochure

Have you visited anywhere interesting while on holiday? Such as a museum, an interesting town or a strange landmark? Or maybe you would like to go somewhere strange or interesting? Think carefully about what the place would be like to visit.

- With your helper design a brochure to advertise your chosen place. Think about:

- what happens there;
- what services are offered;
- when it is open;
- how people can get there;
- how much it costs to get in;
- anything else you can think of.

- Make sure your brochure looks interesting and will make people want to visit this place.

To the helper:

- Help your child to select a place.
- With your child look at other brochures and talk about how they are designed and what they contain.
- Visit the library or travel agent to get information from books and to look at other holiday guides if necessary.

Being able to select relevant information and then presenting this information in different forms is a valuable skill. It is also important to be able to complete research and translate information into your own words.

_____ and
child

_____
helper(s)

_____

did this activity together

Holiday activities

To the helper:

- Talk with your child about different possible summer treats and help them answer the questions if necessary.
- It may help to look through a recipe book or in a shop's deep freeze to get ideas for the ingredients and suggested storage methods. Encourage your child to be original!

This activity can stretch a child's imagination and focus their attention on the vocabulary related to food and 'cool treats' in particular.

_____and

child

_____

helper(s)

_____

did this activity together

Summer treat

If you could invent a brand new, never before eaten, 'one of a kind' summer treat, what would it be?

What would it taste like?
What would it look like?
How would it need to be stored?
What are the ingredients?

- Think of something special.
Then design a container and label it with the information that answers the questions above.

Holiday activities

impact WRITING HOMEWORK

A place of my own

If you want to be alone what kind of special place would you choose?

- Draw a plan of your special place. What would it look like? What would it be built of?
- Make a list here of all the things you'd need to make this special place feel like home.

To the helper:

- Talk with your child about the things they may want to have and help them to edit their list. Is everything essential? What if they had to carry everything there by themselves? Is there anything they could really do without.

This activity requires creative thinking to plan the ideas, and list-writing skills to compile the final list.

_____ and
child

_____
helper(s)

_____
did this activity together

impact WRITING HOMEWORK

Holiday activities

To the helper:

- Find some old newspapers to look for interesting words and phrases that could be combined to make funny headlines.
- Encourage your child to use a writing style that resembles actual newspaper language for their article.

This method for finding a title for a story relieves the child from thinking of something to write about and helps to stimulate the imagination. Writing in different styles is a useful tool for developing writing skills.

_____and
child

_____
helper(s)

_____
did this activity together

Headline jumble

Make up a funny headline for a newspaper story!

- Get a stack of old newspapers, look through them and choose a selection of words from headlines. Look for interesting words, funny words, long words and short words. Cut out the words or phrases which you've chosen.

- Try to put your collection of words together to make some funny or interesting headlines.

For example: **Runaway horse robs bank for carrots.**

- Now try to write a newspaper article to match your brilliant headline!

The same story

- Get two different newspapers for the same day. Choose a story which is in both papers: a person winning an award, a fire, a crime story or any other story.

- Look at the two different versions of the story and compare them. Is everything written in the same way? Have any of the facts changed?

If any of the information is different why do you think this is?

To the helper:

- Supply two papers for the same day and help your child select a story. Read the articles together and talk with them about how they are different.
- Suggest possible reasons as to why the stories may be different: different reporters, witnesses not saying the same thing each time or different witnesses.

Children will see that different sources can present the same information in entirely different ways. They will also see that just because something is in print it may not necessarily be entirely accurate.

_____ and

child

_____

helper(s)

_____

did this activity together

Holiday activities

To the helper:

- Remind your child that abbreviations are often written in capital letters.
- Dictionaries will quite often give lists of abbreviations, and charities and public service groups often use abbreviations for names.

This activity focuses attention on initial letters and word formation. It also highlights the manner in which new words sometimes enter our language.

_____ and
child

_____
helper(s)

did this activity together

Holiday activities

Abbreviations

Abbreviations are words that are made up by shortening a single word or by using the first letter from each of a group of words. For example:

AA – Automobile Association

- Look at these abbreviations which you may have seen:

PTA, USA and FBI.

- Find out what the letters stand for in these abbreviations.

- Talk with your family and friends and see how many other abbreviations you can find.

impact WRITING HOMEWORK

'S' is for Zebra

'S' is for zebra because a zebra has **s**tripes.
'M' is for cow because a cow **m**oos.

This is a game for two or more players.

● Take turns giving each other a letter. Instead of thinking of the **name** of something beginning with the letter, you have to think of a **characteristic** of an animal, person, place or thing.

So, if the letter is 'T' you wouldn't say 'T' is for 'tiger' but 'T' is for my bedroom because it is 'tidy'!

impact WRITING HOMEWORK

To the helper:

● Talk with your child about different characteristics that people, places or animals might have.
● Can they fit their letter to the characteristic and not the object? Help them with ideas to get the game going.

This game helps to focus on the use of attributes in descriptive language.

_____and
child

_____
helper(s)

_____
did this activity together

Holiday activities 85

To the helper:

- Read through the rules with your child and make sure they understand the game.
- Help by suggesting categories and act as a judge when teams are comparing lists.
- Remind the children that original answers get more points, so 'cheating' isn't any use!

This game focuses attention on the initial letters of words, helps children expand their vocabularies and encourages lateral thinking.

_____ and
child

_____
helper(s)

did this activity together

Think of a word

This is a game for two or more teams (or two or more players).

- Before you begin, write the letters from A to Z on small pieces of paper and put them into a bowl.

- One team thinks of three categories (such as: girls' names, types of fruit, countries, holidays, musical groups, animals or articles of clothing) and tells the other team the categories.

- The next team (in a clockwise direction) picks a letter from the bowl and shows it to the teams.

- Each team has one minute to write a word for each category starting with the chosen letter. (For example if the letter R was chosen, words for the above categories could be: Rachael, raspberry, Russia, Ramadan, Rolling Stones, rattlesnake and raincoat!)

- After one minute the teams compare their lists. Score one point for each acceptable word and three points for each word that is completely different from the words used by the other teams.

- Now the team that picked the letter selects three new categories and the next team (in a clockwise direction) picks the letter.

- The first team to 50 points wins.

Enjoy the game!

86   Holiday activities

impact WRITING HOMEWORK

Scuba discovery!

- Imagine that you are the world famous underwater explorer Jean de L'eau. You have recently been diving off the British coast and have just made an amazing discovery!

- Write a letter to your cousin, Phillipe de la Terre, describing what you found, where you found it, the condition it is in and what you plan to do with it. You may want to include a picture of your amazing find with your letter.

To the helper:
- Talk together about scuba diving and what it involves. A trip to the local library may be helpful to gather information.
- Encourage them to use their imagination when describing their 'new find' and to use as many adjectives (describing words) as possible.
- Help to draft a letter following the correct letter writing format.

Descriptive writing of this nature helps children to stretch their imaginations. Letter writing is currently an under-used form of communication.

_____ and
child

_____
helper(s)

_____
did this activity together

impact WRITING HOMEWORK

Holiday activities 87

To the helper:

- It may help to look at other comics for suggestions for character, descriptions and layout and dialogue suggestions.
- Help your child produce the comic in order for it to look as professional as possible!

Comics are super for practice in sequencing ideas, following plot and character development and allow children to use their artistic skills.

_____and
child

_____
helper(s)

_____
did this activity together

88 Holiday activities

Comic book hero

● Invent a character for a comic book adventure. Make a careful list of all the characteristics: appearance, likes, dislikes, attitudes, and any other information which could be important.

● Use this information to produce your own comic book. Carefully illustrate your work and include speech, information boxes or bubbles and 'sound effects'. Make your comic as exciting as possible. Share it with your friends.

impact WRITING HOMEWORK

Comparing newspapers

Have you ever looked at how different words are used in different newspapers?

- Gather together a selection of newspapers from the same day. Try to get a local paper, a tabloid and a broadsheet newspaper.

- Choose one article and make a tally of the word lengths (cross the words out as you go).

- Look for all the one letter words first, then the two letter words and so on. Make a tally showing the lengths of words used.

- Compare the tallies for the different paper's articles.

Is there a difference between the papers? Which paper used the longest words? Which paper used more short words? Why do you think there is a difference?

- Talk with your family and try to work out why some papers use more long words than other papers.

To the helper:

- Talk with your child about why the different papers use words of different length. Do tabloid papers use shorter words more often than the broadsheets? How do local papers compare?

Different papers do use words of different length on average. The papers tend to use word length and reading ages related to their intended reading audience. It is important for childen to realise that different reading levels are all around them.

_____and

child

_____

helper(s)

_____

did this activity together

To the helper:

- Talk with your child about the main points of the story. Discuss what parts must be included and what can be left out.
- Another idea is for you each to write a story with a set title (again using only 50 words), see how your stories are different.

It is important to be able to identify the main events in a story's plot and distinguish between essential and non-essential information.

_____ and
child

_____
helper(s)

_____
did this activity together

Keep it short!

- Choose one of your favourite stories or fairy tales. It's probably quite long isn't it?
- See if you and your helper can rewrite the story using **only** 50 words!

Include all the important parts of the story, but use only 50 words.

90 Holiday activities

impact WRITING HOMEWORK

Where are they going?

Have you ever looked up at an aeroplane in the sky and wondered where the passengers are going? Why they are going there? What they will do when they arrive?

- Write a poem describing the journey, the reasons for travel and possible activities once they have arrived.

Remember that poems do not have to rhyme!

To the helper:

- Help your child group their ideas into stanzas (paragraphs) and add adjectives (describing people, places and things) and adverbs (describing verbs). Encourage them to be as creative as possible and remind them that poems do not always rhyme.

Expressing thoughts and dreams, even daydreams, is an important purpose for writing. Poetry is a form of writing that lends itself well to collecting short thoughts and ideas.

_____and
child

_____
helper(s)

_____

did this activity together

Holiday activities

To the helper:

- Talk with your child about their choice of person to write to and the questions they might ask.
- Encourage them to think of original questions.
- Try to get an address and post the letter. (Books shops and libraries often have books that give addresses for famous people.)

Letter writing is an important skill, and one that is quickly being lost in this age of telephones, faxes and jet travel. Practice of this type gives children an insight into this highly personal form of communication.

_____and

child

_____

helper(s)

_____

did this activity together

Holiday activities

Only three questions!

Think of someone you really admire!

- Write a letter to your chosen person (it could be a rock star, a great artist or the Prime Minister).

What three questions would you ask them?

- Write your letter and post it if you have an address to send it to!

impact WRITING HOMEWORK

No place like home!

Imagine that you have been hired by the local council to design a brochure about your local area that will encourage people to visit.

- Think carefully about your area's good points. It may be helpful to look through the phone book, street maps and other brochures and visit the library and Tourist Information to gather information about where you live.

Is there any important historical information that should be included? Any interesting places to visit?

- Make your brochure as attractive and as easy to read as possible.

To the helper:

- Help your child with the research for their brochure. Visits to the library and local places of interest will provide added information as well.

Research and publishing skills are important to develop for use later in school life.

_____ and
child

_____
helper(s)

_____
did this activity together

Holiday activities

To the helper:

- Look through newspapers with your child and discuss the language used in the articles. How are they different from ordinary speech and writing?
- Remind them to keep this 'journalistic' style as they write.

Making posters and writing extended captions is another form of writing skill to add to their repertoire of writing forms.

_____ and
child

_____
helper(s)

did this activity together

Local hero

Pretend that you have just done something **very** brave.

● Draw a photo of yourself doing your brave deed and write a short newspaper report describing what you have done.

DOWNDERRY ECHO

Acronyms

Acronyms are words that are made up from the first letters of other words.

For example LASER – Light Amplification by Stimulated Emission of Radiation

Some other Acronyms are: NATO and SCUBA.

- Can you find out what the letters stand for in these words?

- Talk with your family and friends and see how many other acronyms you can find. Make a list here.

Acronym	Meaning

To the helper:

- Remind your child that acronyms are often written all in capitals.
- Dictionaries will quite often give lists of acronyms. Charities and public service groups often use acronyms for names.

This activity focuses attention on initial letters and word formation. It also highlights the manner in which new words sometimes enter our language.

_____ and
child

_____
helper(s)

_____
did this activity together

impact WRITING HOMEWORK

Holiday activities 95

IMPACT schools

We are trying to compile a list of IMPACT schools so that we can:
- inform you as new materials are produced;
- offer help and support via our INSET office;
- find out the spread of this type of shared writing homework.

Also, because it is helpful if you have support and advice when starting up a shared homework scheme, we have a team of registered in-service trainers around Britain. Through the IMPACT office we can arrange for whole day, half day or 'twilight' sessions in schools.

I would like further information about IMPACT INSET sessions.

YES/NO

Please photocopy and cut off this strip and return it to:

The IMPACT Office,
Education Dept.,
University of North London,
Holloway Road,
London N7 8DB.
0171 753 7052

Teacher's name _____
School's name _____
Address _____
_____
_____
LEA _____

Management

Most teachers send the shared writing task as a photocopied sheet included in the children's **Reading Folder** or in their IMPACT **Maths folder**. Remind the children that they may use the back of the IMPACT sheet to write on. Before the activity is sent home, it is crucial that the teacher prepares the children for the task. This may involve reading a story, going over some ideas or having a group or class discussion. Some ideas are provided here in the Teachers' Notes for each activity. The importance of this preparation cannot be overstressed.

Many of the tasks done at home lend themselves naturally to a display or enable the teacher to make a class-book. A shared writing display board in the entrance hall of the school gives parents an important sense that their work at home is appreciated and valued.

The shared writing activity sheets can be stuck into an exercise book kept specifically for this purpose. Any follow-up work that the children do in school can also be put into this book. As the books go back and forth with the activity sheets this enables parents to see how the work at home has linked to work in class.

Non-IMPACTers

We know that parental support is a key factor in children's education and children who cannot find anyone with whom to share the writing task may be losing out. Try these strategies:
- Encourage, cajole and reward the children who bring back their shared writing. If a child – and parent/carer – does the task haphazardly, praise the child whenever the task is completed, rather than criticise if it does not.
- If possible, invite a couple of parents in to share the activities with the children. This involves parents in the life of the school as well as making sure that some children don't lose out.
- Some schools set up 'writing partners' between children in two different classes pairing a child from Y6 with a child in Y1 for shared writing activities, perhaps weekly or fortnightly.

None of these strategies is perfect, but many parents will help when they can and with encouragement, will join in over the longer term.

Useful information and addresses

The IMPACT shared maths scheme is running successfully in thousands of schools in the UK and abroad. The shared writing works in the same way, and obviously complements the maths very well. Both fit in with the shared reading initiatives (PACT or CAPER) which many schools also run. The OFSTED Inspection Schedules require and take account of schools working with parents as well as the quality of teaching and learning. IMPACT receives positive mentions in inspectors' reports.

Further information about the IMPACT Project and IMPACT inservice training for schools or parents' groups can be obtained from: The IMPACT Project, School of Teaching Studies, University of North London, 166–220 Holloway Road, London N7 8DB.

The Shared Maths Homework books can be obtained from Scholastic Ltd, Westfield Road, Southam, Warwickshire CV33 0JH.

For IMPACT Diaries contact: IMPACT Supplies, PO Box 126, Witney, Oxfordshire OX8 5YL. Tel: 01993 774408.